W9-AUB-925

THE CAESARS

By the same author

Documents of Liberty
Dark Age Britain

As Beram Saklatvala

The Christian Island
Arthur: Roman Britain's Last Champion
The Origins of the English People

Poems

Devouring Zodiac
The Choice
Phoenix and Unicorn
Air Journey

Translations

Ovid on Love
The Poems of François Villon (Everyman's Library)
Sappho of Lesbos

Henry Marsh

THE CAESARS

The Roman Empire and Its Rulers

St. Martin's Press   New York

937
MS

118597

Copyright © *1971* by Henry Marsh

All rights reserved. For information write:
St. Martin's Press, Inc., *175* Fifth Ave.,
New York, N.Y. *10010*
Printed in Great Britain

Library of Congress Catalog Card

Number 72–79779

First Published in the United States of
America in *1972*

AFFILIATED PUBLISHERS :

Macmillan & Company, Limited, London
– also at Bombay, Calcutta, Madras and
Melbourne – The Macmillan Company of
Canada, Limited, Toronto

I · JVLIVS CAESAR AND AVGVSTVS

Establishing the Empire -
First Century BC

During the 100 years preceding the birth of Christ two great changes took place in the Roman world—the transformation from city state to empire, and from republic to principate.

Rome was originally a small town, built as a result of several tribes coming together for mutual defence. Secure behind their massive walls, the Romans set up their city and lived prosperously under their kings. Later they invented many legends to explain their origins and found a hero, Romulus, after whom they claimed their town had been named.

From the first they showed a genius for military affairs, being as skilful with the sword as with the plough and as steadfast against their enemies as were their own stout walls. They became masters of the lands round about, forming alliances and making conquests until they were rulers of most of northern and central Italy. Then, coming into conflict with Carthage, the great north African city, they seized Sicily and so grew to be a European power.

During the first century BC they carried their arms to the Rhine, took the whole of Gaul, crossed the Channel and entered

Britain. Spain they already possessed, and the lands of the Near East also saw the standards of the legions. Rome became mistress of all western Europe and of part of Asia Minor. It was Julius Caesar who conquered Gaul, and so laid the foundations upon which the complex structure of her European supremacy was built

The second change was from republic to principate. Two men contributed to this, Julius Caesar and his great-nephew, Octavius. The former set up the rule of one man within the framework of the republic's constitution. His work was based on force of arms and the pitiless pursuit of power. The latter, whose work was subtler, less violent and more enduring, formally set up the principate.

To understand the revolutionary changes they wrought, we must first examine methods of government within the Roman Republic.

In 510 BC the Romans destroyed their ancient institution of kingship; sickened by royal arrogance and tyranny, they resolved never again to accept the rule of one man. Instead, they set at the head of the Republic two equal sovereigns, the consuls, who held office for one year. Decisions had to be unanimous and, therefore, each could veto the other. Rome saw this as a defence against the abuse of power by one man, and a safeguard against the revival of a monarchy. But as government by a committee of two inevitably led to delays, the senate was given power to pass 'The Ultimate Decree', in times of peril, formally declaring the state to be in danger and appointing a single head of state with the title of 'Dictator'. The office was tenable for one year, during which the dictator could take those swift decisions which times of war or social crisis demanded

All political power was theoretically vested in the Senate and people of Rome (*Senatus Populus Que Romanus*), and the initials SPQR became the emblem of the City's sovereignty. The Senate was not a fully representative body, members being drawn only from certain families (patricians). The powers of the people (plebeians) were exercised through their *Comitia*

CONTENTS

PREFACE

The name of Caesar was originally borne by a family which, though of senatorial rank, was by no means eminent in Republican Rome. One of them, Gaius Julius Caesar—soldier, politician and statesman—brought immortal lustre to the name. He vastly extended Rome's territories, carrying the Roman eagles into Gaul and being the first to lead a Roman army into the island of Britain. In Rome itself he achieved total power and was appointed dictator for life.

After his assassination by political opponents, men realised how his strong rule had relieved the Republic from the burden of civil war. He was formally declared a god, and his authority in the state was inherited, not without a struggle, by his great-nephew Octavius, whom he had posthumously adopted as his son. Octavius was later given the name Augustus, the Revered One, and created first citizen of the state. He claimed to be the restorer of the Republic, but was in fact the founder of an empire, creating a monarchy almost by stealth. He ruled Rome for many decades, and by the time of his death the citizens had grown accustomed to political power lying in the hands of the Caesars—first of Julius Caesar and then of Augustus. To provide the continuity which Rome demanded, every subsequent Emperor bore the name.

Neither the name nor its glory ended when Rome fell to the Goths in the summer of 410. So great was its magic that it

Boundary of Roman Empire
Modern political boundaries

0 50 100   200   300 miles

U   S   S   R

NLAND

DACIA

RUMANIA

ESIA

Danube

BULGARIA

THRACIA

BYZANTIUM NICOMEDIA

ACEDONIA

GECE

ATHENS

HAIA

BLACK   SEA

BYTHNIA

GALATIA

CAPPADOCIA

ARMENIA

CASPIAN SEA

MEDIA

T   U   R   K   E   Y

ASIA

CILICIA

ASSYRIA

MESOPOTAMIA

Tigris

I   R   A   N

CRETE

CYPRUS

SYRIA
SYRIA

I   R   A   Q

Euphrates

N   E   A   N

LEBANON

ISRAEL
JERUSALEM

JORDAN

ARABIA
PETRA

RENAICA

EGYPTUS

E   G   Y   P   T

S   A   U   D   I

A   R   A   B   I   A

outlasted Constantinople's eastern Empire and became part of
the vocabulary of medieval and modern Europe. The Hapsburg
rulers of the Austrian empire used the title of Kaiser until
their downfall in the 1914-18 war; the Czars of Russia derived
their title from the same source, as did Kaiser Wilhelm II of
Germany, who died in Holland towards the middle of this
century. The name spread beyond Europe, and the Emperor of
India was known as *Kaiser-i-Hind*.

What manner of men were they who bore the name in
Rome and gave it immortality? How did they achieve the
rank of emperor? There is no single answer. Down to Nero,
each was kin to Julius Caesar or Augustus by blood or by
marriage. Thereafter there was no blood link. Some achieved
power by constitutional means, being appointed by the Senate;
some through intrigue; others by bribing the troops; many by
force of arms; and others by popular acclaim. From time to
time brief dynasties were set up: Vespasian and his sons after
him, the Flavians, ruled in Rome; the descendants of Bassianus,
high priest of Syria, sat for a while in the house of Caesars;
and the sons and nephews of Constantine had their day.

The style of the office varied with its holders: some
emperors were content to live simply, as private citizens holding high office; but others loved pomp and luxury. Finally
there came a fundamental change: what had been the supreme
magistracy in a republic became an unashamed and flamboyant
monarchy, in which the emperor's person was considered
sacred and he himself cut off from the activities of mortal
men.

This book is an attempt to tell in small compass the story
of all those men, from the time of Julius Caesar to the sack
of Rome, who bore or claimed to bear the name of Caesar,
and to show how the traditions of Rome came back to
medieval Europe from Constantinople. Because the book is
written primarily for English-speaking people, I have naturally
given prominence to events in Britain. Many of the Caesars
visited the island. Julius Caesar's expedition to Britain, the
frustrated intentions of Augustus, the expeditionary force
under Claudius, the visits of many later emperors, and the

creation of emperors in Britain—all these events are fully discussed. Some have been given rather more detailed consideration than is strictly proportionate in the context of the Caesars'
lives; and in the later period I have sometimes used events in
Britain to illustrate similar events elsewhere. But this book is
not a history of Roman Britain, it is the story of the Caesars.

The book is divided into six sections. The first five deal
respectively with the first century BC and the first, second,
third and fourth centuries AD, though the chronological
divisions do not precisely follow the centuries. Just as the nineteenth century did not truly die until August 1914, so it was
with the Roman world, and I have taken appropriate land-
marks to mark the beginning and the end of each century. The
sixth section deals with events in Constantinople after the fall
of Rome. There the name and title of Augustus endured for
many centuries. There the traditions of Rome persisted, remote
from and almost unknown to the western world. The Crusades
brought Constantinople and medieval Europe into contact and
finally into conflict. So it was from Constantinople, which had
become their repository, that Roman traditions flowed back
into western Europe, to create the Renaissance through which
the work of the Caesars entered the modern world.

H.M.

or Assemblies of Citizens, which elected magistrates and passed legislation. The procedures in the *Comitia* invited considerable gerrymandering. The Romans, as already said, were originally drawn from several tribes; their separate identities had long been lost, but each citizen was still nominally enrolled in one of them, and the tribes formed the constituencies of the Assemblies. Decisions were taken by a majority of the tribes, and within each tribe by a majority of those present in the City and voting. Farmers in the countryside could not regularly attend, so the urban population had a disproportionate influence, to the advantage of tribes with large numbers in Rome. Rich men, when they freed slaves, could enrol them in their own tribes, thus manipulating the voting.

The tribes elected special officers called Tribunes, whose persons were sacred and who could veto any bill. This was devised to provide legal means of blocking any action contrary to the wishes of the common people. Ironically, it was this very office of Tribune which was ultimately to be used to destroy the Republic.

To express the conflict between the privileged senatorial families and the common people, Rome borrowed two phrases from Greece. Some Greeks, like Plato with his conception of the philosopher kings, held that a state should be ruled by the best of its people, and this form of government became known as aristocracy, from the Greek word ἄριστος meaning the best. Others believed that power should lie with the common people, the δῆμος and this form was known as democracy. The Romans translated both words into their own tongue—*optimus*, best; *populus*, people—and by the first century BC there were two clear parties in Rome, the *Optimates* who stood for government by the aristocracy, and the *Populares* who stood for the common people.

The Julian family, which bore the cognomen of Caesar, was of senatorial rank. In the first century BC the head of the house, Gaius Julius Caesar, attained the office of Praetor, an important but not outstanding magistracy. The family, notwithstanding its senatorial rank, had linked itself with the Popular Party, whose leader, Gaius Marius, had married Julia, sister to the head of the family. Marius was a man of common birth, ruthless and able. The family heir was the Praetor's son, also called Gaius Julius Caesar, who was to become Rome's leading citizen and was to dominate his own age and the memories of Europe for centuries. Though heir to a senatorial family, he was thus a nephew (through his Aunt Julia) of Marius, and so linked with the Popular Party.

We know little about his infancy. His mother reputedly gave birth to him after a surgical operation that is still called a Caesarian section. During his childhood his uncle Marius was supreme in public affairs, governing brutally, setting his lust for power above the niceties of legal procedures; but some accomplishments shine through the tyranny of his career, including a reorganisation of the Roman army. Before his day men served for one campaign, without pay and with no long training. Marius signed men on for twenty years and paid them, thus transforming a levy of part-time soldiers into a skilled professional army that was to hold the frontiers of civilisation for many ages. He had other, less admirable, achievements to his name. He manipulated the constitution and his election as Consul for a second term was utterly irregular—first he was absent from the City when elected; second, the constitution forbade two consecutive terms of office. But because of his popularity he was able (again irregularly) to become Consul each year until 100 BC, the year when Julius Caesar was born.

Marius provided many lessons for his nephew: that political power could be won by securing the esteem of the army; that the acclaim of the people was worth more than the support of the Senate; that a man determined to retain power could with impunity brush aside the provisions of the constitution. Towards the end of his life Marius, by now nothing but a tyrant, appointed Julius, then only thirteen, to be *Flamen Dialis* (a priest of the state religion)—a mark of signal favour, for a young man did not normally hold office until he was fourteen.

The boy had in the meantime become engaged to Cossutia, daughter of one of the Knights of Rome, the financiers, traders and merchant adventurers of the City; his father may have planned to improve the family fortune by this match. Then when Julius was fifteen Marius died, aged seventy-three, widely hated for subjecting Rome to an oppression as cruel as that of the hated kings of legend. The Popular Party was swept from power. Sulla, leader of the Aristocratic Party, was appointed dictator, and began the reorganisation of the Republic.

Julius' father died when he was sixteen, and he was left in a different and dangerous situation: Marius alive had been a protector; dead, he was a haunting peril, for many were prepared to take revenge for ancient wrongs upon the dead tyrant's defenceless nephew. Sulla was now governing the City with brutal cruelty. The Republic was sick; judicial murder, tyranny and bloodshed were recognised instruments of government, and were widely used against the supporters of Marius. Young Julius Caesar was in special peril for, in forming an alliance with Marius, his father had been seen by some as a traitor to his own class.

At this time of mortal danger Julius took his first independent action, one which must have appeared startlingly reckless to his friends. He broke off his engagement with Cossutia and married Cornelia, daughter of Marius's old friend and ally, Cinna, thus ostentatiously calling the attention of the ruling Aristocratic Party to his close connection with the execrated Marius. Some say he was in love with Cornelia and that passion made him defiant, others (more plausibly) that he was moved by political motives. Should Sulla fall from power (which in that turbulent Republic was surely inevitable), the Popular Party would be short of supporters of senatorial rank to fill the higher offices. But Sulla was all-powerful at the moment and his reaction was predictably violent. He summarily ordered Julius to divorce Cornelia. The boy was in no position to refuse, but refuse he did—and risked death in so doing. Sulla stripped him of his priesthood, of the dowry he had received, and of his family inheritance. Julius left Rome as a fugitive, escaping Sulla's police sometimes by stratagem, sometimes by bribing his way out of difficulties.

He still had powerful friends. The Vestal Virgins and some of his relations interceded with Sulla, who reluctantly agreed

B

to forgive him, but added prophetically that the young man would one day destroy the Aristocratic Party, for, as he put it, 'In Caesar there are many Mariuses!'

In 81 BC, aged nineteen, Julius joined the army and served in the Near East under Marcus Thermus. For saving the life of a soldier in action at Mytilene on the island of Lesbos, he won an oak-leaf crown, one of the most coveted of Roman decorations. Later he was transferred to Cilicia where he saw further service, learning much of legionary discipline and of the moods and attitudes of the troops. His military career, lasting for some three years, was marred by one scandal. Marcus Thermus had sent him on a mission to Bithynia, to collect a fleet from its king, Nicomedes. Julius stayed with Nicomedes longer than either decency or his mission required. The king, said rumour, fell in love with the handsome young soldier and a homosexual relationship developed; the stories redoubled when he visited Bithynia a second time and Julius was never allowed to forget this dubious adventure; years later, after he had become famous, stories and comic songs about the incident still circulated.

Dolabella, against whom Julius brought a prosecution for extortion, referred to him as a 'rival to the Queen of Bithynia'. Curio called him 'Bithynia's brothel'. Julius was once referred to in an official edict as 'The Queen of Bithynia'. It was said that he was 'a man who lusted after a king and who now lusted to be one'. Finally, when he was granted a Triumph in Rome for his conquest of Gaul, some barrack-room wag wrote a marching song which has been preserved:

Caesar laid into Gaul, Nicomedes laid into Caesar,
See now Caesar in triumph, he who laid into Gaul!
Nicomedes has no triumph, although he laid into Caesar!

The Roman world saw homosexuality as a matter for ribald laughter. But that the stories lasted so long suggests that Caesar took no strong measures to refute them; perhaps he knew that it would endear him to his soldiers, emphasising him as a man with human feelings and a devil-may-care attitude to conventional morality.

In 78 BC, when he was twenty-two, news came of Sulla's death; the long reign of the Aristocratic Party was over and the prize of power could now be grasped by others. One man, Marcus Lepidus, had already sought unsuccessfully to seize it by force of arms. This was no time for an ambitious young man to be serving in the remote provinces of the East; the dangers and opportunities of Rome beckoned, and thither Julius went. He at once set about securing popularity and, through it, authority. After the revolt of Marcus Lepidus had failed, Julius brought an action for extortion against Cornelius Dolabella, who had once held the supreme office of Consul. For an unknown young man to prosecute so eminent a personage was reckless and audacious, but Julius was impatient to win the acclaim of the masses. He failed to obtain a conviction and, according to Suetonius, discreetly left Rome for Rhodes. There he studied under Apollonius Molo, a distinguished professor of rhetoric (Cicero was one of his students). Plutarch tells us that in later life Julius was accounted second of all the orators of Rome and might have stood first had he not preferred to seek pre-eminence in arms.

It was then, says Suetonius (though Plutarch places this incident earlier) that Julius was captured and held to ransom by pirates who demanded the huge sum of 20 talents for his release. Young Julius with a typical flash of arrogance, laughed at their proposal and promised a sum nearer to his true worth, namely 50 talents! While his messengers were obtaining the money, he remained with the pirates on shipboard for over a month, accompanied by one friend and two servants. Defenceless and isolated, he refused to be browbeaten. Much of his time was spent in writing; he read his work to his captors and, when they failed to show a proper admiration, berated them as ignorant barbarians. He promised that he would see them all brought to justice and crucified; wiser men than the pirates would have knocked him on the head forthwith, but they did not know the abilities lying behind the arrogance, and laughed at such engaging impudence.

Caesar was released when the money arrived, but the pirates, no doubt delighted to have the cash and to be rid of an insolent and awkward prisoner, had not seen the last of him. He secured a ship from a neighbouring port, attacked and defeated them and, fulfilling his grim promise, crucified them all, leav- ·ing them to die in slow agony. Incidentally, he also recovered the ransom money!

Returning to Rome and to the advancement of his ambition, Caesar—like his uncle Marius—threw in his lot with the Popular Party, seeking to build a political career upon the votes of the Assemblies rather than of the Senate; and it was the former which promoted him to the rank of Prefect, the equivalent of Colonel. He was appointed Quaestor in 68 BC. In the following year both his wife Cornelia and his aunt Julia died, and he delivered the funeral orations, which was usual. But the words he used about Julia were not. He seized the occasion to mark not his private grief but the splendour of his royal and divine descent. Suetonius reports this passage from his speech:

> Her mother [Julius's own grandmother] was descended from kings—the regal Marcians, a family founded by the Roman king Ancus Marcius. Her father was descended from gods. For the Julians (to which clan we Caesars belong) count descent from the goddess Venus. So Julia's family can claim both the sacred power of kings who reign supreme among mortal men, and the worship due to gods, who hold kings themselves under their authority.

These were strange words to use in republican Rome, where ineradicable odium attached to the name of king. They were stranger still coming from a supporter of the Popular Party, for Julius was not merely claiming royal descent but proposing that kings, by divine right, should reign supreme among mortals. Some might already have wondered whether this arrogant young man's ambitions soared higher than any office in the Republic, whose future overthrow he might one day contrive.

Now free to make a second marriage, he chose Pompeia, daughter of Quintus Pompeius and a grand-daughter of Sulla. Was this purely a marriage of political convenience to give him a footing in the Aristocratic Party in case, after all, they might prosper? If so, it was ill-timed. Revulsion against Sulla had been growing. He had diminished the authority of the Assemblies, permitting only the Senate to initiate legislation; and he had restricted the powers of the Tribunes, the spokesmen and guardians of the common man.

In the provinces some followers of Marius still clung to their offices. One, Quintus Sertorius, had defended his governorship of Spain by force of arms, defeating all the armies sent against him. In 77 BC (when Julius was twenty-three) the Senate sent to Spain a young officer named Cnaeus Pompeius, known to history as Pompey. Although he had previously held no senior office, Pompey was given full command and four years later Sertorius was brought down. Pompey returned from Spain in 71 BC. He was granted a Triumph, riding in glory through the streets of Rome at the head of his victorious troops. Later he and Crassus, one of Rome's wealthiest citizens, were elected Consuls. This was the result of a compromise, Pompey representing the Popular Party and Crassus the Aristocratic Party.

After instituting such popular reforms as the restoration of the Tribunes' powers and the purging of the Senate of some of the worst of the dead Sulla's nominees, Pompey looked about him impatiently for new paths to greatness. In 67 BC he was given supreme command over the Mediterranean with orders to clear the sea of pirates. Julius supported the appointment. Three things were now obvious to him: first, political power often went to a successful soldier, be he Marius, Crassus or Pompey; second, that Pompey's absence from Rome provided a golden opportunity for another leader to emerge; and third, that the way to greatness lay through the support of the common people.

Julius now had a further taste of foreign service, this time in Spain; but his appointment had none of the glamour of Pompey's, for he served as a travelling magistrate. It was said that he saw a statue of Alexander the Great in a temple there and mourned that, at an age when Alexander had conquered the world, he had as yet done nothing memorable. Shortly thereafter he returned to Rome, impatient to emulate

Alexander. He continued to back Pompey who, once supported by the Aristocrats, was now the nominee of the Popular Party. Caesar endorsed Pompey's appointment as Commander-in-Chief of an expeditionary force to be sent against King Mithridates of Persia; he knew that a successful campaign would enable Pompey to win further renown, but felt this was a price worth paying for Pompey's absence from the City, which would allow his own ambitions more freedom.

To win the acclaim, and with it the political support, of the people he drew Marius's reputation from the shadows of contumely, reminding Rome of the dead leader's achievements. An image of Marius was displayed during the funeral ceremony of his widow, Julia; and Julius began to be seen as his dead uncle's political heir. But as yet the oak-leaf crown he had won in his youth had given place to no laurel. Now in his thirties, some of the bright promise of his youth had faded. Pompey, only six years older than himself, had already achieved the Consulship, a Triumph, and an outstanding naval and military command. Julius now acted quite outrageously. The towns beyond the River Po had long demanded the same civic rights as those enjoyed by all other Italians. To those cities Julius travelled, and advised them to take direct action, rejecting the slow processes of constitutional argument. He came perilously close to leading a revolt and to marching against Rome as a rebel, backed by an army of malcontents seeking their rights at the sword's point. Swift action by the Consuls, who sent reinforcements to the region, preserved the peace and saved Caesar from the disgrace which such action would have attracted.

In 65 BC, now aged thirty-five, he was appointed Aedile, or magistrate in charge of public buildings. He used the office to gain popularity, and Cicero wrote that, while still an Aedile, he planned to become a monarch. There were, in fact, rumours that he and three other men planned to rise in the Senate and kill as many senators as possible, seizing power for themselves. These rumours cast the first shadow on Julius's reputation—a shadow that was to culminate in the dark night of his assassination.

There was a further suspicious sign: one of an Aedile's duties was to put on a show of gladiators, but Julius collected so many swordsmen that he was suspected of recruiting a private army. The Senate passed a special bill limiting the number of gladiators that any man might keep in the City.

Recognising the Senate's hostility, Julius tried to work through the Assemblies, and there sought the Governorship of Egypt. The wheatlands of the Nile delta were the granary of Rome; whoever commanded Egypt might not only achieve military glory but gain effective control over Rome itself. But again the Senate blocked him.

With major appointments eluding him, Julius now sought the office of *Pontifex Maximus*, high priest of the state religion, an office which carried an aura of ancient sanctity. He was lavish in his bribery, incurring such huge debts that failure would have brought him financial ruin. On the morning of the election he kissed his mother goodbye, saying that if he did not return as *Pontifex Maximus* he would not come back at all. His gambler's throw succeeded, the Assemblies of the People giving him an overwhelming majority.

When the Cataline conspiracy came to light in 62 BC, Caesar for the first time faced physical violence in the Senate chamber. The Senate angrily clamoured for the death sentence on Cataline, while Julius, by now Praetor, demanded the lesser penalty of banishment. By procedural obstruction he almost prevailed, until some of the Knights of Rome, whose task it was to maintain order, advanced upon him with drawn swords. Julius then wisely withdrew and attended no further sessions that year.

He continually acted in defiance of the constitution, sometimes to his peril. His first act as Praetor was arbitrarily to take the work of restoring the Capitol from the man to whom it had been entrusted and to give this task to his friend Pompey. Only when the Aristocratic Party demonstrated violently in the streets did he give way. Later, with a friendly tribune, he tried to force certain controversial bills through the Senate. Both were suspended, but Julius unlawfully continued to preside over the courts, and only when warned that he would be removed by force did he doff his official robes and withdraw.

In the following year, he obtained his first major overseas appointment, as Governor of Further Spain. This was a minor prize compared with Pompey's Mediterranean command, for the success of which he was again awarded a Triumph. Julius rode quietly through the olive groves and villages of Spain, his victories yet to be won and the plaudits of his troops yet to be earned. His departure to his command had been hasty, some said to escape his creditors! Then in one swift campaign he subdued the mountain tribes of Lusitania, captured the city of Brigantium, and returned to Rome in the summer, briskly demanding the consulship and a Triumph. The latter was denied him but he was elected Consul with Marcus Bibulus as colleague, and soon established himself as the dominant partner. There was a wry joke that documents were now dated 'During the Consulship of Julius and Caesar'!

There were now three leaders in Rome: Pompey, whose victories had won him the designation of *Magnus*, 'The Great'; Crassus, whose vast wealth gave him immense influence; and Julius, whose military skill had now been proved in Spain and whose popularity with the people was unchallenged. If civil war was to be avoided an alliance was inevitable. So in 60 BC, when Caesar was forty, the First Triumvirate was formed. All three undertook to oppose any legislation of which any of them disapproved. The alliance was cemented by the marriage of Julius's daughter Julia to Pompey, and for a while the Triumvirate provided Rome with a stable government.

The provinces were always governed by former Consuls who, after holding office, retained their powers outside the City; as ex-Consuls (or *Proconsules*) they represented Rome's sovereignty. A man's proconsular appointment was announced when he was elected Consul, giving him time to study his new territory, to select staff and appoint congenial lieutenants. The Senate tartly expressed its disapproval of Julius's Consulship by nominating him Proconsul in an unimportant region of Italy, where he would be nothing more than a forestry warden and superintendent of farmlands. But he had the decision vetoed by a friendly tribune. The baffled Senate still avoided giving him any command overseas and granted him instead the governorship of Cisalpine Gaul, the lands south of the Alps. Then the Governor of Transalpine Gaul (lying to the north of the Alps) died suddenly, and the Senate awarded Julius that province as well. So in 58 BC Julius, now forty-two, took command of both the Gauls and Illyria (the modern Yugoslavia). Large areas of his new territories were still unconquered. Julius now had the opportunity to show his mettle by subduing nations which had not hitherto felt the weight of Roman arms.

In 57 BC Pompey's proconsulship was extended for five years and he was given control of the City's corn supply, but he and Crassus became rivals for the command of an expedition to Egypt. Julius also faced opposition: Ahenobarbus, a candidate for the consulship in 56 BC, announced that if elected he would cancel Julius's appointment and withdraw him from Gaul. In order to revive the flagging strength of the Triumvirate, Julius invited his two colleagues to meet him at Luca, some 120 miles north of Rome, where the alliance was reaffirmed. Plans were laid for the future and Pompey and Crassus were next year elected Consuls.

Meanwhile Julius's military reputation grew as victory followed his eagles in Gaul. He brought to the battlefield the same ruthless audacity which he had earlier displayed. In victory he could be merciless, and he makes no attempt to hide this in his own writings: for example, he butchered every man, woman and child of a nation that had surrendered after long resistance; and ordered the right hand of every man and boy of another tribe to be hacked off so that they might never again stand sword in hand against Rome. The portraits on his coins make these stories credible: in the lean cheeks, furrowed harshly from nostril to chin and in the thin-lipped mouth, we can see something of the qualities that were to take him to the summit of power and thence to a bloody death. But ruthlessness alone would not have earned him the golden reputation which he now began to enjoy. He won not only the confidence but the affection of his troops, marching and fighting with them, at once a grave commander-in-chief and a gay fighting companion. Once when a legion was nearly broken, with almost all its officers dead, he joined them and rallied the surviving officers by name, his very presence bringing a renewal of courage.

He always showed a close interest in the background of his enemies, and collected information not only on their military methods but on their religion, their social structure and national characteristics. It is to him that we owe something of our knowledge of the Druids, the priests and sages of the Celts; he wrote that their religion was probably indigenous to Britain and had been taken thence into Gaul. During the years 58 and 57 BC, Julius fought his way northwards until all Gaul was occupied.

He had an able second-in-command named Labienus. The two campaigned together for many years but Labienus was later to die fighting against his one-time friend. With Gaul subdued the whole of western Europe lay under the sway of Rome, from the sun-drenched shores of Spain to the River Rhine, and from the blue Mediterranean to the misty waters of the Channel.

The Romans were the best infantrymen in the world—disciplined, steady and invincible, but they had neglected the cavalry arm and had few substantial mounted units. The Gauls were renowned for their horsemanship and, accordingly, Julius enrolled many into his army, with their own chiefs as officers. The policy was risky, for these men were but newly conquered. Whatever the glamour of serving in the Roman army, in their hearts they remembered the grievous wrongs that Rome had inflicted upon their peoples. They had been overcome and enslaved for no better reason than Rome's assumption (personified in Julius) that she had a natural right to govern the whole world.

Believing that his campaign of pacification was completed, Julius left for Illyria. His confidence was misplaced. Requisition of supplies by the garrisons reminded the Gauls of their subjection, and inflamed the smouldering ashes of their resentment. Soon all Gaul was in flames and Julius had to hurry back. He fought the rebels by land, and along the Atlantic

coast by sea, thus gaining some experience of combined operations.

In the following winter the Germans once more invaded
Gaul. Julius despatched a punitive expedition across the Rhine
to demonstrate to the Germans the invincible weight of Roman
arms. In the summer of 55 BC he took another of his
seemingly reckless decisions, resolving to commit an army
to the perils of the narrow seas and to invade the unknown
island of Britain. His motives were twofold. First, he had a
soldier's curiosity to learn what lay beyond his front. As he
wrote, he 'believed it would be of great value to him to land
in the island, to ascertain something about the people there,
and to obtain some knowledge of the land itself, its ports and
havens'. Second, the Britons had continually assisted his
enemies; when the Gauls had revolted, the Britons had sent
them reinforcements. The island moreover provided a haven
for fugitives. We are reminded of the 1940s and that
Julius was not the last conqueror to realise that no armies
can successfully hold western Europe unless they occupy
Britain.

So Julius began his preparations, gathering as much military
intelligence as possible. There was considerable trade between
Britain and northern Gaul, so he summoned and questioned
many merchants, trying to discover the size of the island, the
strength of its kingdoms, and the national character and
military methods of the Britons. He tried to identify the main
ports, hoping to find a harbour suitable for a large invasion
fleet. The merchants gave away little or nothing, and Julius
admits that he obtained no information of any value from
them.

Volusenus, one of his officers, was ordered to reconnoitre the
coast of Britain but he merely sailed along it without landing.
Julius had assembled his invasion forces somewhere near
Boulogne. There he gathered his transports and the ships he
had used in fighting the Gauls on the Atlantic coast. Such
massive preparations could not be hidden from the Britons.
They sent a delegation to ask why an armed invasion was
planned and offering peace. Julius reassured them and they

returned to Britain accompanied by Julius's representative, a Gaulish noble named Commius. Julius's warlike reputation had already crossed the Channel, but the Britons, despite all they had seen of a great army preparing for war, were neither cowed nor despairing. They assembled their armies, which contained large squadrons of swift war chariots, for which they were famous.

When all was ready Julius's fleet put out on the night tide. For the soldiers sheltering behind the bulwarks the adventure was an eerie one, such as no Roman army had hitherto undertaken. As they adjusted their packs and weapons, their excitement was sharpened by an underlying apprehension of the unknown. Soon this was to shake the iron discipline that had carried them victoriously across hundreds of miles of hostile country. In the lands where hitherto they had fought there had been roads and tracks along which they could retreat, and over which reinforcements could come to their aid. Now a dark waste of sea lay behind them and, as the shores of Gaul receded, so vanished their last links with the known world.

Eighty transports and fighting longships carried two legions and auxiliaries, perhaps 20,000 men. One legion was the Tenth, Julius's crack troops, whom he treated almost as his personal bodyguard; they were to him what the Eighth Army was to Montgomery, or the Old Guard to Napoleon. The wind stood fair and, as their course lay northwards, the first glimmer of dawn split the sky to starboard. The sense of solitude and desolation increased. No land was visible, only the grey ring of the dawn horizon surrounding a hostile sea. As the light grew, at about nine o'clock, the lookouts saw white cliffs rising starkly from the shoreline of foam. On the green turf surmounting the cliffs troops of Britons were clearly visible. Julius realised that to attempt a landing there would be to invite disaster; no soldiers could storm those sheer cliffs. On the beaches they would be at the mercy of arrows and missiles from above. Julius ordered the fleet to turn to starboard and stand a little out to sea, and the men watched the grim coastline slip past them as the fleet sailed up the coast. The sun rose higher and the morning chill faded from the wind. The Britons cantered along the cliff tops keeping pace with the ships. Then the lookouts saw a long beach, sloping gently towards a shingle ridge and thence, without defence of cliff or headland, to a green countryside of pasture and cornfield. Down to the water's edge rode the British cavalry, spears grimly poised. The Roman transports were of too deep a draught to be run ashore and had to stand off. To leap into the chill sea, their hands cumbered with sword and shield, into water so deep that to stumble was to drown, was daunting even to those seasoned troops. They hesitated.

Julius ordered the longships to outflank the enemy and to land on their right, where the Britons retreated; but their centre held and the legionaries still hung back in the transports, restrained by the deep water and their mounting fear. Then the standard bearer of the Tenth Legion raised its bronze eagle and called out: 'Come on men, jump—unless you want to hand over the eagle to the enemy! As for me, I'm going to stand by the Republic and our leader!' He leapt into the water. Those beside him followed. To left and to right, men on the other transports jumped into the sea and waded ashore. Confused fighting followed with soldiers from different units assembling to form an improvised line. Soon, enough troops had struggled ashore for a charge to be mounted and the Britons retreated. Julius could not order the enemy's pursuit, for his cavalry still lay in Gaul. They had sailed from further down the coast and had been swept back by the tide. Most of his horsemen were Gauls, and we may speculate whether accident or secret defiance had delayed them.

After the battle a delegation from the defeated enemy came to sue for peace. With them came Commius, Julius's envoy, who said he had been captured on arrival and put in irons, and that the Britons after their defeat had freed him and brought him thither. Was his story true? What coincidence kept him so close to the fighting that he could appear immediately thereafter (*statim* is Julius's own word) in the guise of mediator? It is significant that three years later Commius commanded a massive Gaulish army which waged relentless war against Julius. After an interval he led a second war of liberation and was defeated, whereupon Volusenus sent a mission ostensibly to parley but in fact to assassinate him. They bungled their bloody work, wounding him (as they thought mortally) in the head and Commius, recovering, swore that never again would he look upon the face of any Roman. Later, in a cavalry skirmish he gave Volusenus a spear-thrust through the thigh, taking fair revenge for his own treacherous wound. Years later Commius fled from occupied Gaul to Britain and there became king of the Atrebates. Gold coins with his name, *Commius Rex*, have been found in Hampshire and Berkshire. His sons and grandsons became kings after him. In the light of these later events, we may surely believe that he was already deceiving Julius; perhaps he had been with the Britons following the fleet's course from the steep cliffs to the shelving beach. Once they had failed to throw the Romans back into the sea, he may have counselled them to break off the engagement and to conserve their forces for a later battle.

Four days after the landing a storm broke. Julius's cavalry, who had again set sail, were driven back. Worse, most of the invasion fleet was wrecked on the beaches. Without supplies, their means of retreat shattered, the troops faced the bleak prospect of a starving winter in a hostile island. Urgent orders were given to repair the ships and for corn to be gathered from the surrounding countryside, where the ripe harvest shone under the golden September sun. The Britons, hearing of the disaster, broke the fragile truce. A party of the Seventh Legion was ambushed while collecting the reaped grain, their arms laid aside, and many were killed. It required a desperate sortie from the camp, led by Julius himself, to rescue them.

During the next few days the Britons received reinforcements from neighbouring regions and finally took the offensive. They were beaten off by the legionaries, now impregnably entrenched round the perimeter of their camp. But the action showed that the initiative now lay with the Britons, and Julius took no further risk. That same afternoon he ordered the evacuation and the soldiers sailed back to Gaul with little accomplished. The speed of their evacuation is a measure of the expedition's failure.

The legions on the transports, wearied with long days of marching and fighting, saw with relief the grey coast of Gaul looming ahead, but it proved no safe refuge. The local tribes had grown restless during their absence; the first men to land were attacked and had once more to fight their way to safety. Julius left the quelling of this revolt to Labienus. As the aim of his British campaigns had been to win a reputation similar to Pompey's wherewith to dazzle the citizens, and thus to consolidate his political position, he returned to Rome. Before leaving, he ordered Labienus to build a fleet to sail against Britain in the following summer. He drew up new specifications for the transports: they were to be broader in the beam, of shallower draught, and the bulwarks were to be lower. The tackle was to be obtained from Spain, and work was to go ahead with all speed.

In Rome he was well received. The Senate voted a public holiday in his honour lasting an unprecedented twenty days. He could now account himself Pompey's military equal as he knew himself to be his political superior. The acclamation of the people was a sweet augury for the future.

Pompey had again been appointed Commander-in-Chief in Spain with ten legions, which he kept in Italy—nominally for training. In fact, his purpose was to dominate Rome with these troops and to ensure the City's continued acceptance of the Triumvirate. Crassus was given command in the East to subdue the Parthians. Thus, when Julius returned to Gaul, all three of the Triumvirate were absent from the City, each warily watching the others' intentions.

When Julius rejoined his army in Gaul, he found that the building of the new fleet had gone superbly well: 600 transports awaited him with 28 fighting longships. These, with the ships he already had, gave him a total of some 800 vessels.

First he had to grapple with unrest in Gaul. One of his Gaulish cavalry officers, Dumnorix, tried to avoid joining the British expedition, advancing numerous pretexts including his religion. When compelled to join, he slipped out of camp with some of his troops, but he was pursued and surrounded. Defiantly crying out that he was a free man, he was cut down and slain by his pursuers.

Resolving not to repeat his earlier failure, Julius embarked not two legions but five and 2,000 horse. The orderly embarkation of so many men (the equivalent of five modern divisions) and the marshalling of 800 ships indicate the complex and deft organisation which now controlled the Roman army. The units boarded the transports, the horses stepping nervously up the gangways. Sails were hoisted as the sun sank on the port quarter, and the fleet moved northwards into the gathering darkness. At midnight the wind dropped and the ships drifted with the tide. At dawn the lookouts reported that they were off course, the enemy coastline lying to port. Sails were lowered and the troops were ordered to row towards the same beaches where they had disembarked in the previous year. They made an unopposed landing at midday. The Britons, intimidated by the vast fleet, which covered the Channel as far as the eye could see, decided not to fight it out on the beaches.

Immediately on landing the legionaries began to dig in. At midnight, eighteen hours after sailing, and after their labours of rowing and digging, the main body of troops marched inland under Julius's personal command. By daybreak they had penetrated 12 miles. A successful action was fought for a river crossing against the cavalry and chariots of the Britons; these retreated into a hill fort, which the Seventh Legion successfully stormed, avenging their comrades who had died in last year's ambush. Next morning three legions resumed the advance to re-establish contact with the enemy. But then came news from the beaches that last year's destruction of the ships by storm had been repeated. Julius hurried back and found about forty ships a total loss and many others damaged. He sent despatches to Labienus ordering further ships to be built, and had the vessels on the beaches drawn up beyond the tide and surrounded by a fortification. All this took about ten days. He then returned to his main army, which he led towards the Thames. Against him stood Cassivellaunus, King of the Catuvellauni and Commander-in-Chief of the Britons. The mounted Britons harassed the advancing army, inflicting many casualties. Cassivellaunus organised a defence in depth, so that any breakthrough by the Romans met renewed resistance in the rear, but finally the legions fought their way across a ford of the Thames. Cassivellaunus disbanded his main army and thereafter waged a guerilla war. Julius now allied himself with the Trinovantes, the most powerful nation in south-east Britain. Mandubricius, a prince of the Trinovantes, had earlier fled from Cassivellaunus and sought refuge with Julius. The tribe were thus natural allies. But Cassivellaunus in his turn sought allies in Kent, enlisting the help of the four kings who reigned there, and, with their forces, assailed the beach-head camp. The attack was beaten off and Cassivellaunus sent a peace mission to Julius, who decided to risk his armies no further. Giving generous terms to his enemy, he embarked his men and returned to Gaul after spending only a few days on the island. Because of the shortage of ships he evacuated his troops in two separate journeys, successfully and without loss. The brief time he spent seems sadly disproportionate to the magnitude of his preparations.

The reputation that Julius won in these campaigns was out of all proportion to his achievements: his first expedition was a total failure, involving severe losses of men and ships; the second was little more than a moderately successful punitive expedition ending in evacuation. His misjudgement of Commius may have contributed to his failure, as did the lack of resolution shown by Volusenus on that first reconnaissance. But, perhaps most of all, the cruel oppression under which Gaul now laboured nerved the Britons to a stubborn resistance. They knew that no reinforcements could reach the legions, and that to succeed they had only to hang on and to keep their armies in being.

On his return to Boulogne, Julius had to face a rising tide of revolt and a growing Gaulish liberation movement. It was not until 49 BC that Gaul was truly settled, after a campaign marked by terrible brutality. But in Rome Julius now enjoyed a brilliant reputation. His sword had brought the whole of

C

western Europe under Roman rule, he had marched beyond the Rhine into Germany and had ventured into Britain, which no Roman army had visited before. If his main motive in going to Britain had been political, it had succeeded triumphantly, despite his military failure.

From Rome came the grave news that the influence of the Aristocratic Party, which still mistrusted Julius, was growing and that Pompey was working more closely with it. In 49 BC the Consuls (both nominees of the Aristocratic Party) proposed that Julius and Pompey should relinquish their commands, but Pompey refused and Julius stayed on in Gaul.

It was illegal for any general to lead his troops out of the area of his command, but knowing Julius's character, the Senate was fearful that he would defy the law and march his legions from Gaul into Italy, seizing power by force of arms. They consulted Labienus who, though a trusted officer of Julius, supported them; but he assured them that the armies of Gaul would always remain faithful to the constitution. To make doubly sure the Consuls appointed Pompey their deputy for the defence of Italy, and the Senate decreed that Julius should be relieved of his command. His friend Mark Antony, now a tribune, vetoed the bill but the threat remained.

Julius was now in Cisalpine Gaul (northern Italy) with the Thirteenth Legion, on the river marking the boundary between his province and Italy proper. In 49 BC, realising that Pompey's appointment endangered his whole career, he defied the law and crossed the river—the Rubicon. Like so many of his actions, this was a gambler's throw. Indeed, as he watched the Thirteenth Legion cross, he said to his friends, 'The dice are thrown'.

He divided his single legion into flying columns, seizing two of the cities held by Pompey's forces whose garrisons came over to him. Within weeks Pompey and the two Consuls evacuated Rome, seeking refuge in Capua, and Julius's army, now grown to three legions through the defection of Pompey's men and new recruitment, entered it. His troops were in high spirits and one of the songs they sang is still preserved:

We bring our general home again
A bald old fornicator he!
Lock your wives at home, you Romans
If you'd have them safe and free!

Ten weeks after the fighting had begun, Pompey left Italy
and crossed into Illyria. He had ten legions in Spain, but he
was not there to lead them. Julius marched into Gaul and led
his legions into the Pyrenees, defeating Pompey's forces. While
he was in Spain, the Senate appointed him Dictator, in order
to supervise the election of the Consuls. He and one of his
officers were duly elected.

Pompey, after the defeat of his lieutenants in Spain, drew
reinforcements of men and treasure from the East. The
Adriatic was patrolled by his fleet, commanded by Julius's one-
time colleague Bibulus. Pompey was relying upon a long war:
his army was larger, his wealth greater, and he hoped to wear
away the resistance of his rival. But at the Battle of Pharsalus,
Julius's 20,000 veterans routed the 40,000 who followed
Pompey; 15,000 were killed in the pursuit and Pompey's forces
were utterly destroyed. Pompey himself fled by sea, first to the
island of Lesbos and thence to Alexandria in Egypt. As he
stepped ashore, he was murdered by a Roman centurion.

Julius was now sole ruler of the civilised world. In pursuit
of Pompey, he had landed in Egypt with two legions, their
numbers reduced by casualties to some 3,000 men. But with
this tiny force he took charge of the complex politics of
Egypt.

When Alexander the Great died without an heir, the
provinces of his empire were divided among his generals. One
of these, Ptolemaus, became king of Egypt and his descendants
still reigned. They had adopted Egyptian customs and each
Ptolemy married his own sister, so that the crown descended in
the pure line. When Julius landed, the boy king Ptolemy XII
was about to attack the armies of his elder sister Cleopatra,
while another sister waited in armed neutrality to back the
winner. Julius threw in his lot with Cleopatra, imprisoned
Ptolemy XII and gaily defended her palace in Alexandria

against the boy king's 20,000 troops. Here was an adventure after Julius's own heart, fighting in a strange land, recklessly delaying his return to Rome where power lay. He took a personal part in the fighting. If the stories are to be believed, he worshipped not only Mars but Venus; and passion spiced the adventures of war. He and the young Cleopatra fell in love. After he had defeated Ptolemy XII, Cleopatra was duly married to Ptolemy XIII; but the son she bore was named, not Ptolemy, but Caesarion!

In 47 BC, after two years, he returned to Rome. His friend Mark Antony was in command there, but the city was in disorder. Julius was once again appointed Dictator. He still had to mop up centres of Pompeian resistance, including an army in North Africa led by his old second-in-command, Labienus, who later crossed into Spain, where he mustered thirteen legions. Julius led eight legions against them and Labienus died in battle, fighting stubbornly against his old commander.

Julius was appointed Dictator once more in 46 BC (when he enjoyed four Triumphs) and again in 45 BC; finally in 44 BC he was appointed Permanent Dictator (*Dictator Perpetuus*). It was clear that the Republic had ceased to exist. The office of Dictator, designed to be filled only in an emergency and to be held for one year, had been bestowed upon Julius for six consecutive years, and finally for life. The Aristocratic Party was in disarray, with its last champion, Labienus, dead on a blood-stained Spanish field. The Senate, anxious to placate the all-powerful Julius, showered honours upon him: for example, they ordained that he might wear every day the formal Triumphal dress, including the laurel wreath, which was so dangerously close to a crown; and his portrait was allowed to appear on coins. He was in all but name King of Rome, and Emperor of all western Europe and of large tracts in the near East and North Africa.

Some Romans foresaw with dismay the establishment of a new monarchy. In 44 BC, during the feast of the Lupercalia (the festival of the she-wolf who had suckled Romulus), Mark Antony offered Julius a royal crown. This was no doubt a device to test public opinion and it was clear that the crowd, in spite of their affection for Julius, was shocked. Wisely, he refused it. But for all that, he was in fact a monarch, and there were many in Rome prepared to defend the Republic against the tyranny of any monarchy, whether declared or tacit. Chief among these was Caius Cassius Longinus, who had served as one of Julius's deputies in Spain. Another was Marcus Junius Brutus, an intellectual and a descendant of that Brutus who had helped expel the former kings of Rome centuries before. (Some said he was Julius's illegitimate son.) These men, with others, resolved to restore the Republic at all costs. The paths of constitutional redress being blocked, their only means was assassination and to this end they plotted.

On 15 March 44 BC Julius went to the Senate and took his seat, where the conspirators came and greeted him. One of them, Cimber, presented a petition which Julius waved aside, and Cimber laid a hand upon his shoulder. Julius protested impatiently and they all rushed upon him with their daggers; he took twenty-three wounds before he died. Some say that with the instincts of a soldier he fought against his assailants, using his bronze pen as a pathetically ineffective weapon. Then, when Brutus struck him, he called out, 'You, too, my son?' and gave up the struggle and so died.

Suetonius tells us that he was tall, fair complexioned, sturdily built and had brown eyes. He suffered occasionally from epileptic fits, but was as hardy on campaign as he was dandified in civilian life. He had many love affairs: with Servilia, mother of Brutus; with Cleopatra, as we have seen; and with Eunoë of Africa. He was a moderate drinker but a great spendthrift. He fought and bribed his way to power, but he failed to understand that the people of Rome were not ready to accept the rule of one man, in spite of the turmoil into which the Republic had sunk, still needing those republican forms of government to which they were devoted. His invasion of Britain was a vital step along the road to absolute power, for he had to offer the people military achievements at least equal to those of Pompey. He had matched the latter's brilliant Spanish campaign with his own wars in Gaul,

and countered his rival's naval successes in the Mediterranean
with his own more dramatic crossing of the narrow seas, to
fight in the strange island lying in the far north. Before his day
Britain was as mysterious to the Roman world as Africa was
to eighteenth-century Europe—a country only reported in the
exaggerated tales of travellers and seafarers. So Britain paradoxically entered recorded history because of a political
struggle waged hundreds of miles from her steep cliffs, in a
distant city built upon seven hills.

Rome reacted to Julius Caesar's assassination with hysterical
anger, the people expressing their grief in rioting and violence
against the assassins. Mark Antony, his former friend and
colleague, assumed authority in the disordered city.

Julius left no constitutional heir to his political power nor
any children to inherent his personal wealth. His nearest kinsman was Octavius, a great-nephew, son of his niece Atia. Julius
had advanced the young man's career, appointed him to the
Senate and given him minor offices. Octavius was only nineteen when Julius died, and was living as a student in Illyria,
but on hearing the terrible news he hastened back to Italy. His
future was uncertain, for he had neither political experience
nor influence, but at Brindisi there was a portent of future
greatness. The local troops, who revered the dead Julius, acclaimed Octavius by the name of Caesar, anxious that he
should replace his great-uncle in their affections. Octavius
declined the acclamations but the incident must have stirred
his ambition.

In Rome he learned of Julius's will: he was not only the
heir to Julius's immense wealth but had been posthumously
adopted as his son. Accordingly he changed his name to Gaius
Julius Caesar Octavianus, but his position was still perilous.
Mark Antony, self-appointed custodian of the dead dictator's
authority and wealth, refused to pay Octavian his legacy.
However, as at Brindisi, so in Rome. Many army units declared
for him and he was soon able to challenge the powerful
Antony, who had to flee from Rome and retreat beyond the
Alps. Octavian, still only twenty, next compelled the Senate
to elect him Consul. One of his officers, Cornelius, took his

demand to the Senate and, when that august body demurred, flung back his cloak, slapped his swordhilt and said: 'If you will not choose him as Consul, this will do so!' Not for nothing had Octavian inherited the name of Caesar!

He now held the highest office in the state, and the seasoned Antony had to accept the twenty-year-old boy as his equal. Bloodshed would have been the inevitable outcome of a direct clash, with Octavian and Antony turning their swords upon one another in destructive rivalry. But a leading soldier, Lepidus, reconciled the two men and Rome drew back from the brink of civil war. The three of them, disregarding constitutional forms, constituted themselves into a Committee of Three (known to history as the Second Triumvirate) to govern Rome and her provinces.

They first decided to destroy all who might oppose them. Cold-bloodedly they made a list of those who were to die, using terror as an instrument of policy: 300 senators were slaughtered, including Cicero, and over 2,000 knights of Rome were executed. The triumvirate filled their war chests with the confiscated property of their victims and Rome, numb with shock, accepted their total authority.

In the following year (42 BC) Octavian and Antony hunted down Brutus and Cassius, scattering their armies at the battle of Philippi. With Brutus and Cassius dead, the hopes of those who had sought to destroy the tyranny of a monarchy, and to restore the Republic, finally vanished.

After renewed friction and a further dispute and reconciliation, the three men divided the Roman world between themselves. To Lepidus were given the North African provinces; to Antony, Egypt and the East; and to Octavian, Rome, Italy and the West. All the world knows how Antony fell in love with Cleopatra, Queen of Egypt, whom the great Julius Caesar had loved at Alexandria and whose son she had borne. To please his queen, Antony carved out an independent empire based on Egypt, invading Judea and other eastern lands. A final struggle between Octavian and Antony for the mastery of the world became inevitable, though there was an attempt by the two men to come to terms. As part of the settlement Antony married Octavian's sister, Octavia. Later emperors (Caligula, Claudius and Nero) sprang from these two, so that Antony's descendants later ruled over the Empire.

Antony later put Octavia aside and the rivalry between him and Octavian turned to open war. The Republic perished in a naval engagement, fought off the promontory of Actium, between the combined fleets of Antony and Cleopatra and the ships of Octavian's general Agrippa, in September of 32 BC. Cleopatra's nerve failed and her ships precipitately retreated, and Antony, now more lover than commander, followed. Their fleets were broken. As the wreckage of the broken galleys sank beneath the waters, the 500 year old Republic vanished with them. Antony committed suicide. Cleopatra, rather than suffer the indignity of being made a prisoner, followed his example, dying (as the world remembers) from the bite of an asp smuggled to her by a faithful servant, to give her the ease of death and the reward of immortality.

On his return to Rome Octavian celebrated a triple Triumph and then, in 27 BC, modestly informed the Senate that he would lay down his special powers and retire into private life. The Senate, dreading the return of civil war and longing for the stability that resulted from a single ruler, declined his offer—as he had probably foreseen. With insistent modesty he announced that he had restored the Republic. He refused all powers except those of a tribune, which he accepted for life. This tribunitian power was the foundation upon which he built his position as Emperor. For now his person was sacred, he had a veto in the Senate and could initiate legislation.

Later the Senate granted him the name of 'Augustus'—the August or Revered One; in an inscription Octavian recorded that the name had been given 'because of my authority'. He was also granted the powers of a proconsul for life. Thus, using the harmless offices of the Republic, he created an Empire. He wore no crown, received his friends as equals, and lived a simple and somewhat austere life. Though he enjoyed a banquet as much as the next man, he was equally content with a meal of bread with raisins or dates. Not for him the ostrich heads and exotic dishes of his successors.

There were of course scandals about his private life. Some said that he shared his great-uncle's homosexual tendencies, though his devotion to women is perhaps the best defence against that charge!

He was administrator rather than conqueror, and sought no new lands. He saw the Rhine and Danube as Rome's natural frontiers, and bequeathed this policy to his successors, who followed it for centuries. Perhaps the Empire would have endured for longer had the legions conquered the lands beyond those rivers. His caution was strengthened by a terrible disaster in AD 9. One of his commanders, Varus, had led three legions across the Rhine on a reconnaissance in force, but they were ambushed in the Teutoberger Forest and totally destroyed. Worse, and to their everlasting disgrace, they lost their eagles. Augustus, grief-stricken, was often heard to say to himself: 'Varus, Varus, give me back my legions!'

There were rumours that he had planned to invade Britain. Cassius Dio, an historian writing about 30 BC, recorded that Augustus thrice planned the conquest of Britain but each time cancelled his plans because of troubles elsewhere. The poet Horace wrote that the Britons, like the Persians, had been subjected to Augustus, but this was flattery, not fact.

In his youth Augustus had become engaged to a young girl, but on his second reconciliation with Mark Antony he married the latter's stepdaughter, Claudia. He divorced her before the union was consummated and married Scribonia, who had been twice married before and was the mother of one child. By her he had a daughter named Julia, but this marriage, too, ended in divorce. Augustus told his friends that the reason was that Scribonia continually criticised his habits! Afterwards he married Livia Drusilla, who was married when he courted her and pregnant by her husband, Tiberius Nero. Scandal said that the child she was carrying was indeed Augustus's. This marriage was permanent and successful but Livia bore him no children. She became a colleague as well as a wife; he exchanged notes with her about state or family problems and always listened to her advice. She turned a blind eye to her handsome husband's peccadilloes, which it was said she sometimes encouraged.

Augustus's daughter, Julia, first married Marcellus, who died in 23 BC. She then married Agrippa, Augustus's great general and his designated heir; she bore him five children and the future of the house seemed assured. In 12 BC Agrippa died, and Augustus had to seek another successor. At Livia's insistence (and some said reluctantly) he chose his stepson Tiberius, who married Julia in the same year; but ten years later she was banished on charges of immorality to the island of Pandataria where she died.

The future lay with Tiberius, for Augustus's grandsons, Gaius and Lucius, died young. (Some said that Livia, jealous for Tiberius's future, had a hand in their death.) Agrippa Postumus, the third grandson, was banished to an island and the seed of Augustus survived only through his grand-daughters.

Augustus grew old in the service of the state, keeping the peace, reforming the laws, giving judgements with good humour and commonsense, appointing governors or generals and patiently organising the empire. Rome, in gratitude, showered honours upon him. *Pontifex Maximus*, Father of his Country, many times Consul—he embodied in his own person the traditional dignity and simplicity of Rome, her efficiency and her gravity, and something of her gaiety. He attended the games in the arena, played for money with his friends after dinner and—if Suetonius is to be believed—often indulged his taste for pretty women.

The end came in AD 14. He had begun his struggle for power at the age of nineteen and was now seventy-four. Looking back over the years, he was conscious of having played his part successfully on the world's stage. Quoting a tag that actors used at the end of a play, he turned to the friends and attendants standing around his bed, and said, 'If I've played my part well, give me a round of applause!' He gave his signet ring to Tiberius, thus nominating him as heir to his authority, and so died.

The pretence that Augustus was the highest officer in a republic died with him; he bequeathed Rome and her Empire to Tiberius as another man might have bequeathed a farm. The Senate had given Octavian the title of Augustus; he himself passed it as a legacy to Tiberius. The Republic was now dead and the Empire, created by no formal announcement or constitutional instrument, was finally established.

II · TIBERIVS TO NERVA

The end of the House of Julius -
First Century AD

When Tiberius came to power, he added to his own names those of his adoption, and ruled as Tiberius Claudius Nero Caesar Augustus. He was already an experienced soldier. In 20 BC he had seen his first service in Armenia, in a campaign to restore one of Rome's client kings. After a further tour of military duty he was appointed consul in 13 BC and for the next few years was again a commander, subduing the tribes of Pannonia. It was then that his imperial destiny began to be apparent. He was compelled by Augustus to divorce his wife (Vipsania Agrippina, daughter of Agrippa) and marry Julia. Poor Tiberius obediently did so but with great sorrow.

After the ambush of Varus, Tiberius was sent to restore the Rhine frontier and proved a cautious and efficient commander. He supervised every detail of the campaign, living with his troops in the camps and gaining a sound reputation.

He and Julia had adopted Agrippa Postumus, Augustus's third grandson, to provide dynastic continuity. But in circumstances that are not clear (some authorities speak of insanity) the young man was banished to an island.

More and more Tiberius realised that he was little more than a caretaker for Gaius and Lucius Caesar, Augustus's two grandchildren. His disillusionment was strengthened by the increasing notoriety of Julia's immorality. Separated from the wife he loved, married to a public strumpet, and unwilling to continue undertaking perilous adventures to defend a sceptre which others would inherit, he withdrew from public life and lived for a while in Rhodes in voluntary exile. But the two young men died and on the death of Augustus, he succeeded to power, though the succession was not undisputed. There were two plots against him which he put down with cruel efficiency. Also after taking power Tiberius caused Agrippa Postumus, the last surviving grandson of Augustus, to be put to death, so that there might be no rival to his authority.

During his reign, the prefect of the Praetorian Guard became of increasing importance. To Sejanus, who held that office, Tiberius entrusted almost all matters of state. For the first time Rome was governed not by her Emperor but by her Emperor's minister. It was not until AD 31 that Tiberius became aware of Sejanus's shortcomings, and then Sejanus and many of his friends were condemned by the Senate and executed.

While leaving some power in the hands of the Senate, Tiberius finally did away with the authority of the Assemblies and governed more and more as an absolute ruler. In his old age, by now infamous for his cruelty and lasciviousness, he withdrew to the Isle of Capri, leaving the government entirely to deputies in Rome. An account given by Seutonius of his sojourn on the island makes ugly reading. Sexual degeneracy, the exploitation of young men and women (and even of babies), unbridled sadism, and a paranoid fear of his enemies marked the old man's declining years.

It was during his reign that Christ was crucified. From its unpromising beginnings in an obscure province, its founder executed as a common criminal, the faith spread rapidly throughout the Empire. There is an old tradition that Christianity came to Britain during the reign of Tiberius. Among the legends the most notable is that of the shadowy figure of Joseph of Arimathea: after he had offended the authorities by giving burial to the body of Christ, he is said to have sought refuge in Glastonbury, where he built a church dedicated to the Virgin Mary.

In AD 37 Tiberius died, by now hated for his cruelty. Men heard of his death with a sigh of relief. Earlier he had adopted and named as his heir Gaius Caesar, son of Germanicus. Gaius was the great-grandson of Augustus (his grandfather had been adopted by the latter) and also descended from Mark Antony through his grandmother, Antonia the Younger.

The boy's dead father Germanicus had been one of the most heroic figures in the Julian house. Gaius, as a baby, often accompanied his father on campaigns, and became the darling of the troops. They dressed him in a tiny uniform complete with military boots, *caliga*. He was nicknamed *Caligula* or 'little boots', and no one thinks of him by any other name. He succeeded Tiberius while still in his twenties and his reign opened with splendid promise. But it ended in terror, for an innate streak of cruelty became plain madness. He would murder for amusement and torture as a pastime. Some said that he had had a hand in Tiberius's death.

It seems that he prepared an invasion of Britain but nothing came of it. Suetonius tells us he assembled a huge army, which he led to the seashore in northern Gaul; but these preparations for a serious military adventure degenerated into a farce of total insanity. On the beach he drew up his army in line of battle, backed by the great catapults that were the artillery of the day. The men advanced towards the sea, not daring to question the commands of the Emperor. Finally he ordered them to gather seashells in their helmets. These were his trophies, the symbols of his victory over the gods of the sea— if not over Britain!

Because this preposterous adventure is told by Suetonius it must be received with caution. In writing his biographies of the first twelve Caesars, Suetonius was moved by political motives. His book is an essay on the doctrine that power corrupts and that insanity and depravity inevitably come to men wielding total authority; he shows each emperor beginning his reign virtuously and ending by governing viciously. The legend that

lust, perversion, incest and madness were the occupational
diseases of Roman emperors began in his pages. Tacitus, a far
more objective historian, records that Caligula had a modest
and decent bearing, though this concealed a ferocious spirit;
he was impetuous but he had learned from his great-grandfather to be politic in all he did. Tacitus's full account of
Caligula's reign is lost and we have to rely very largely upon
the prejudiced Suetonius, but behind the ludicrous anecdote
of the battle of the seashore there undoubtedly lies a true story
of Caligula's intention to invade Britain. A lighthouse was built
at Boulogne during his reign; and Tacitus in his *Agricola* is
specific that Caligula planned an invasion.

The attack on the sea was only one example of his madness.
He appointed his horse to be Consul! Once he said that he
wished the entire Roman people had but one neck so that he
might behead them all at a stroke. After three years of terror,
in AD 41 he was assassinated by two officers of his guard, one
of whom, Cassius Chaerea, had been goaded beyond endurance
by Caligula's obscene taunts. Cassius was a seasoned soldier
and Caligula was for ever hinting that he was a homosexual,
giving him as the watchword each night phrases referring to
his supposed effeminacy. The butchery of Caligula was
clumsily done and the poor mad emperor died horribly and
slowly. At first people were afraid to believe in or to rejoice at
his death, lest he himself had spread the rumour in order to
smell out disloyalty and to slaughter all who exulted. Once the
fact was established, however, there was open joy. Many,
sickened by recent tyranny, wished to re-establish the Republic,
but events moved too swiftly for them.

In the mad young emperor's household there lived his
elderly uncle, Tiberius Claudius Drusus, brother of the well
loved Germanicus. When he heard of the murder, he feared
that the soldiers might slaughter all Caligula's family (they had
already murdered his wife), and hid timorously behind the
curtains on a balcony. A legionary, wandering through the
deserted palace, saw Claudius's frightened feet protruding
under the draperies and dragged him out. Claudius, terrified,
knelt and begged for mercy. To his surprise and horror the

legionary saluted him as Emperor! He was taken to the palace guardroom, whence the soldiers carried him in a sedan chair to their barracks in the city. To the bystanders he seemed overcome with despair and fear. In the general disorder no one in the streets paid much heed to the chair or the soldiers; nor had they any inkling that this was the improbable procession of a new emperor. They beheld the old gentleman with the same compassion they would have given to an innocent man being carried away for execution, which many thought to be the case. Meanwhile the Consuls and the Senate had called out the City troops who seized the Forum and the Capitol, their purpose being to prevent the election of a new Augustus and so to restore the Republic. Claudius spent an anxious night with the soldiers. If the Senate was successful, then by allowing himself to be declared Emperor he would become the first traitor to the newly restored Republic. Should the republicans fail, and should he too stubbornly resist the nomination of the soldiers, he would have offended the army and grim indeed would be his future.

Studying his past, no one would have considered him capable of making so difficult a decision in so short a time. He was born in France in 10 BC and already mature when Augustus died. Because of his disabilities he had not been treated with the honour due to a member of Augustus's family. After his brilliant brother's adoption by Tiberius, Claudius became head of his own family and took the honoured name of Germanicus, but he was pathetically different from his heroic elder brother. A sickly boy, he grew up an ailing youth, despised as stupid by all the family. He dragged one foot, his head lolled to one side, he dribbled when upset, and had a severe stammer. Perhaps he was what today we would call a spastic. Augustus, intent always upon projecting the glamour of his own authority and the importance of his family, was embarrassed by such a kinsman. Letters from him to his wife Livia have been preserved by Suetonius, one of which reads:

My dear Livia,
    I have spoken with Tiberius, as you asked me, as to what should be done with your grandson, Tiberius Claudius, during

the Games of Mars. Each of us agrees that we must now reach
a decision as to what policy to follow about him. For if he is
(if I may so put it) not lacking in any way, and is in full
possession of his faculties, then why should we have doubts
about taking him through the same career and promotions as
those through which his brother was taken? But if we feel
him to be stupid, or mentally and physically disabled, then he
would merely provide material for derision, both against
himself and ourselves, by the public which is always ready to
laugh at this kind of thing. We shall continually be in difficulty if we consider the matter on each separate occasion
and do not clearly decide whether or not he can hold public
office.

However, for the present, on the matters we have discussed,
I would not find it disagreeable for him to preside over the
priests' dinner party during the Games of Mars if he allows
his kinsman, Silvanus's son, to be by him, to guide him and to
make sure that he does nothing that could make him conspicuous or invite derision. But I would find it disagreeable for
him to watch the Games from the Imperial Box, as he would
become conspicuous if placed in front of the auditorium. I
would also not like him to go to the Alban Mount, or to be in
Rome during the days of the Latin Festival: for if he can
follow his brother to the Mount, why should he not become
City Prefect himself?

So, my dear Livia, you now have my views—namely that
we should decide something right away, and not fluctuate
between fear and hope.

When Claudius came of age, he was still kept under the care
of a tutor. Perhaps as compensation for his disabilities and for
being deprived of all the benefits due to his rank, he took
to writing (an art which even the sickliest and most dull-witted
may pursue). Augustus's wife Livia was a dominating woman.
It was possibly she rather than Augustus who tried to shut
this unhappy boy out of the family circle. Certainly Augustus,
in a further letter, proposed that he might see a little more of
the lad:

I shall indeed invite young Claudius (who is now growing up)
to supper every day while you are away, so that he doesn't

D

dine alone with his friends Sulpicius and Athenodorus. I do wish he would now be more careful and less impulsive in choosing a friend to imitate in the way he moves, carries himself and walks. The poor boy is most unfortunate, for on important topics, where his mind doesn't go a-wandering, he shows clearly a sound character.

Claudius's literary work had not been without effect. However stammeringly he might deliver a speech, his texts were well constructed. On one occasion, after he had struggled through a public oration, Augustus wrote to Livia:

My dear Livia,

Upon my life, I really admired your grandson Claudius for being able to please me so much when reading aloud to me! For I just cannot see how anyone who speaks so defectively can, when reading aloud, say what has to be said so clearly!

Claudius was not totally debarred from the *cursus honorum* (the progression from office to office by which young men of good family obtained training and experience) but was given a minor appointment, as a member of the College of Augurs. This was an ancient priesthood, originally concerned with prophesying from the flight of birds. Nor was he omitted from Augustus's will, where his neglected name appeared among the heirs of the sixth rank.

When Augustus died, Claudius began to have hopes of a place in public life. The Knights of Rome asked him to discuss the funeral arrangements on their behalf with the Consuls. Later he earnestly asked Tiberius for some official appointment. Tiberius sent him the robes of a Consul, with a present of 40 gold pieces. Claudius asked to be given the duties as well as the ornaments of office, but received the biting reply from Tiberius: 'I intended you to spend the 40 gold pieces on playthings for the Saturnalia Festival!'

There were two unsuccessful attempts to find him a wife: first he was engaged to a great-grand-daughter of Augustus, Aemilia Lepida, but a family quarrel prevented the marriage; he was next betrothed to Livia Medullina Camilla, but she died on what was to have been their wedding day. Later he married Urgulanilla, the daughter of a distinguished soldier. But he divorced her when her behaviour became a public scandal and when she was suspected of murder. Next, he married Aelia Paetina, daughter of a former Consul, but this marriage too ended in divorce. Thirdly he married Messalina, an ambitious nymphomaniac, whose sexual adventures became the scandal of Rome. She was executed in AD 48 for plotting against him.

Tiberius, being childless, had to follow Augustus's example and adopt an heir. Tacitus writes that he considered Claudius, which would have been dynastically logical, for Claudius was, after all, his nephew. But he rejected the idea because of Claudius's well known stupidity, and so selected Caligula. Disappointed of public office, spurned for his physical and mental disabilities, isolated from the family circle, Claudius was for years content quietly to pursue his literary labours and to live withdrawn from the politics and intrigues of his family. This was the man, now fifty years old, who stood cowering behind the curtain on the day of Caligula's murder and who was now both prisoner and Emperor of the turbulent soldiers.

Next day the Tribunes summoned him before the Senate to declare his intentions. Claudius declined to go, sending the cautious reply that he was being forcibly held and could not comply. Meanwhile the common people were out of sympathy with the republican aspirations of the senators, being now accustomed to the Augustan system which had freed them from the plague of civil war. For them, the cruelties and depravity of Tiberius on Capri and the insane waywardness of Caligula within the palace were mere rumours. They knew only that for decades the army had fought against foreign foes and the bloody wars of Roman against Roman had long ended. They came on to the streets, flocking to the building where Claudius was held. They shouted their slogans, demanded to have a single ruler and cheered the name of Claudius. The Senate, accepting defeat, formally confirmed him in power. Tiberius Claudius Drusus Caesar was declared Augustus. He gave a bounty of 150 gold pieces to each of the soldiers and in so doing set a precedent; the bounty became common practice and finally the office of emperor was literally put up for auction.

His first act showed a wisdom belying his reputation. He declared an amnesty for the two tumultous days following Caligula's murder. There was to be no witch-hunting and no revenge upon those senators who had planned to destroy the Principate. This swift and generous action averted rivalries and unrest which might well have led Rome back to the bad old days of civil war.

He showed intense loyalty to his family, persuading the Senate to declare his grandmother Livia a goddess, with the title of Augusta, despite the aloof contempt in which she had held him. He celebrated the memory of his brother Germanicus in many ways; one was by issuing a fine bronze coin (a sestertius) showing an equestrian statue of his dead brother surmounting a triumphal arch. Nor was his loyalty limited to the Caesars: he also remembered his grandfather Mark Antony, ordering his birthday to be kept as a public holiday. Having seen at close hand the autocracy of Augustus and the subsequent tyrannies of Tiberius and Caligula, he strove to strengthen the surviving republican institutions, projecting himself simply as a private citizen holding high office. He treated the Senate with respect, asking their ratification for decisions taken by his representatives in the provinces. Wishing to hold a market on one of his estates, he sought the Consul's permission like any other private citizen. He declined to accept the designation *Imperator*, or commander-in-chief, from which our word 'emperor' derives. Neither the engagement of his daughter nor the birth of a grandson was celebrated as a public holiday, as had been usual under preceding Emperors.

He took his magisterial duties seriously. He was now able to fulfil the wish he had expressed to Tiberius that he should discharge the duties as well as wear the robes of office! Suetonius recorded, with obtuse derision, some of his sayings on the bench. In fact he frequently acted with refreshing commonsense. For example, one of the judges (who corresponded approximately with our jurymen) was once challenged by a litigant because he was involved in a case that was to come before the court. Claudius said he would hear the judge's case first, which would give the litigant an opportunity to assess the court's impartiality. Once, when a woman denied that she was the mother of a young man, he ordered her to marry him. Solomon's reputation for wisdom was earned by a not dissimilar ruling. To discourage people who ignored the courts, he always found against absent persons. By many he continued to be held in contempt, was frequently insulted, and at least once physically attacked in court.

He put the government of the Empire on a businesslike footing. He appointed secretaries who formed the basis of a senior civil service and who also acted as ministers: chief of these were Narcissus (whom we shall meet later), Pallas, who looked after money matters, and Polybius. They were all freed slaves and were educated and able men. (Claudius did not share the general prejudice against men who had once endured slavery.) He thus laid a solid foundation upon which a sound administrative system was later to be built.

In AD 43, two years after his accession, he ordered the invasion of Britain. The carping Suetonius wrote that Claudius's one war was a mediocre affair, but, in fact, it was well planned and brought Britain permanently into the Roman Empire, the despised stammerer succeeding where the great Julius Caesar had failed. He chose as commander in chief Aulus Plautius, who had already served the state with distinction and who was now governor of Pannonia. (Plautius's wife, Pomponia Graecina, was charged with following a foreign superstition under Claudius's successor Nero, and there has been speculation whether she was guilty of following the newfangled religion of Christianity.)

Why did the un-military Claudius attempt the conquest of Britain? First he needed some military achievement to reinforce his incongruous position as Emperor; second, Rome required the memories of Augustus's procrastination and of Caligula's failure to be erased by victory; third, there were sound reasons for bringing the island into the Empire. Britain was well known as an exporter of wheat, of slaves and metals and was financially attractive as a province. Moreover the political situation within Britain made the time opportune.

Cunobelinus (Shakespeare's Cymbeline and probably a great-grandson of Julius Caesar's opponent Cassivellanus), ruler of the Catuvellauni in Hertfordshire, Bedfordshire, Buckingham-shire and East Oxfordshire, had died in AD 40. The descendants of Commius reigned in the lands around Silchester with a branch of the family governing Sussex and Hampshire. The Trinovantes, whom Julius Caesar had befriended, still dwelt north-east of the Thames but had been conquered by Cunobelinus, who had probably become overlord of Essex and Kent. Suetonius had referred to Cunobelinus as *Rex Britanniae* or King of Britain, which was not true; but he was assuredly the most powerful figure in the south-east. On his death he left two sons, Togodumnus and Caratacus, who were strongly anti-Roman, whereas the Trinovantes, though conquered, were still friendly to Rome. So the forces of Claudius came to a Britain divided. They had only to overthrow the sons of Cunobelinus and the whole South-east, the most civilised part of the country, would fall to them.

How much of the planning had Claudius done personally? He was an historian, having for some time studied under Livy; and the invasion of Britain was certainly organised by someone who had read Julius Caesar's 100-year-old work. Plautius took four legions: the Ninth (nicknamed the Spanish) from Pannonia, the Second from Strasburg, the Fourteenth from Mainz and the Twentieth from Cologne. Cassius Dio tells us how the troops reacted to the terrifying idea of a campaign in the strange land of Britain: they disobeyed the order to embark, refusing to be taken 'outside the known world'. Plautius remonstrated in vain and reported back to Claudius, who sent his freedman Narcissus to address the men. When Narcissus, an ex-slave, mounted the rostrum, the soldiers were struck by the hilarious incongruity of the situation. They, freeborn citizens, were to be harangued by a former slave! It was like one of the jokes at the December feast of the Saturnalia, when the roles of master and servant were reversed in the general jollity. Some wag in the ranks yelled out the greeting: 'Io Saturnalia'. The tension broke in gusts of laughter, and the troops now followed the orders of their general.

They sailed across the Channel in three divisions. There was an eerie absence of opposition when they landed, and they dug a fortified camp just above the beach at Richborough in Kent. Their trenches have been excavated, so we can still see their handiwork and hear, in our imagination, the bustle of 30,000 men consolidating their position on a hostile but deserted shore. Later a great monument was built to mark the site of the first landing, and it may have taken the form of a lighthouse beckoning the numerous trading ships and transports which later crossed the Channel from Gaul, bringing wine and oil, silverware and glassware, and abundant coin for the legions' pay. The cruciform foundations, built of flint, still stand but the stones of the monument are long since vanished, probably used as building material by the Saxons who later settled round about. Fragments of broken marble have been dug up, with carved letters, but these are tantalisingly insufficient for the inscriptions to be restored.

The legions advanced inland to find the enemy. The two princes, Caratacus and Togodumnus, made their separate stands and were beaten piecemeal, Togodumnus being killed. Next, the army of the Bodunni, probably a Kentish tribe, was defeated and their territory occupied. Meanwhile, behind the now broken screen of their armies, the Britons established their defences along the River Medway. A flanking attack was entrusted to the Second Legion; its commander, Flavius Vespasianus, a tough professional officer of middle class stock, was to win a brilliant reputation in Britain. Plautius ordered him to march upstream and find a ford, and attack while the Gaulish cavalry swam the river and attacked the enemy's front. Vespasian crossed the Medway on the enemy's flank as ordered and attacked, but was beaten back. Next day there was a general engagement and after bitter hand-to-hand fighting the British resistance was broken and the Romans forced the crossing.

The victorious legions then resumed their advance to the Thames, probably reaching London. Claudius had arranged,

once the first phase was successful, to take personal command
so as to be seen as a triumphant military figure. Accordingly,
on the pretext that the Emperor's help was desperately needed,
Plautius now sent for him. Claudius journeyed swiftly to
Britain, by sea from Rome to Marseilles and thence by road to
Boulogne. His 'rescue' of Plautius had been planned in advance;
all his preparations had already been made and he brought not
only reinforcements but even a team of fighting elephants!
Whether his motives were strictly military, to overawe the
Britons, or whether he wanted to add drama to the victory that
Plautius had prepared for him we shall never know. Once
arrived, Claudius took command of the expeditionary force,
scored the victory he needed, then turned eastwards and
captured Camulodunum (Colchester), the royal city of the
dynasty of Cunobelinus.

In Rome there was erected a triumpal arch, and an inscribed
stone from it survives, listing the proud titles of Claudius, Son
of Drusus Caesar Augustus, Germanicus, Pontifex Maximus,
Father of his Country. The stone, offered by the Senate and
People of Rome, records that he conquered eleven kings in
Britain, without any losses, and for the first time brought
under Roman rule barbarian nations dwelling across the ocean.
Britain was Rome's first and only province outside Continental
Europe and Asia or the shores of the Mediterranean.

At least one of the kings submitted peaceably. In
Chichester an inscribed stone was found in the eighteenth
century bearing the name of Cogidubnus Claudius, 'King and
Imperial Representative'. His first name Cogidubnus is Celtic,
and his second name, Claudius, and the fact that he was
appointed imperial representative show that he had collaborated with the occupying power. This is confirmed by Tacitus
who refers to Cogidubnus by name, and who cannot forbear
from commenting that the Romans used even kings as instruments to enslave a people! More vivid evidence of Cogidubnus
has recently come to light. The remains of a massive palace
have been excavated at Fishbourne, just outside Chichester.
The huge building could have been erected only at enormous
cost, and is clearly the work of Roman architects, while its

mosaics show the presence of Italian craftsmen. All this required resources far beyond those of a local king. Was it paid for by the Roman authorities? Was this the price paid to Cogidubnus for placing his people under the yoke of Rome? The size and splendour of the palace seem to justify the sour comment of Tacitus.

After the fighting was over, a new town was built just outside Camulodunum, the old city of Cunobelinus. Here a temple was raised to the divinity of Claudius, probably the first public building in Roman Britain, and on its ruined foundations the Normans later built a castle. It is perhaps the oldest building in Britain still in use, for the Norman castle now houses the Colchester town museum.

Much of what Claudius did in Britain can be deduced. Certainly he was present at the final battle. He would have visited Colchester and, with his interest in history, would have limped with fascinated curiosity through the deserted palace of the dead Cunobelinus. He may also have seen the small town that was London's predecessor, and crossed the Thames by a bridge mentioned by Dio. Maybe he met Cogidubnus, who could hardly have taken the Emperor's name without his personal permission and patronage. Before he left, he appointed Plautius Governor, thus formally creating a Roman province.

Meanwhile Vespasian, who was later to become Emperor, remained in the island commanding the Second Legion. Frequently in action, he was on one occasion surrounded by the enemy and nearly killed. He was rescued by his son Titus (later to become Emperor in his turn), whose troops killed many of the enemy.

In Rome, Claudius was awarded his Triumph and was driven victoriously through the City with his troops. Some of the older spectators must have chuckled to see the palace buffoon, a most unlikely candidate for military glory, riding in the triumphal chariot as proudly as Pompey or the warlike Julius Caesar. To celebrate his victory Claudius put on a gladiatorial show, where many of the captured Britons fought and died. As they stood in the hot sunshine looking upon the laughing and gaily dressed crowds, come in their thousands to see them die, they might well have wondered who were the civilised and who were the barbarians.

After Plautius had completed his term of office, he was replaced by Publius Ostorius. On returning to Rome Plautius was awarded an Ovation, which was a victory parade, replacing the Triumph, which was now reserved for members of the imperial family. Ostorius arrived in Britain as winter was beginning, to find many of the Britons still defiant, raiding the occupied lands and attacking the territories of Rome's allies. Caratacus, last surviving son of Cunobelinus, though defeated, had not submitted. The armies of Plautius had given him little room for manoeuvre. The Ninth Legion had marched north-eastwards to Cambridge and possibly into East Anglia. Another column had advanced into the Midlands. The Second Legion (under Vespasian) had marched westwards, possibly as far as Devon, and almost certainly through the territories of Cogidubnus. By the time Ostorius took over, Caratacus had retreated into what is now Wales. The boundary of Roman Britain was then possibly the line of the Fosse Way, today a main road running from Exeter diagonally across Britain to Lincoln. Caratacus penetrated the frontier outposts and led effective raids into the territories of the Roman province.

Ostorius strengthened this frontier, probably stationing the Second Legion at Gloucester. He secured his rear by settling a group of ex-servicemen at Colchester as a trained reserve, in case of need. This done, he ordered a column to advance into Wales, to attack the forces of Caratacus, which stood securely in prepared positions. The Roman troops stormed the defences, utterly defeating the Britons. The wife, daughter and brothers of Caratacus were captured, but he rode free. The door to the west being locked against him, he travelled north-wards to the kingdom of the Brigantes, who dwelt in what is now Yorkshire, governed by their Queen Cartimandua. (The idea of a queen regnant is very ancient in Britain as Cartimandua and, later, Boudicca remind us.) Cartimandua had made her peace with the Romans and Caratacus, in seeking her help, was gambling desperately, with his life as the stake. His gamble failed. Cartimandua imprisoned him, chained him, and handed him over to the Roman army. With his capture, organised resistance to the Romans collapsed. It was to be another decade before the Britons waged further war against them.

Caratacus was sent to Rome and led through the streets as a public show. Tacitus records the scene: first marched his captured servants and bodyguard; next were displayed the great collars and torques (probably of gold) which he once wore, with the booty he had taken from the Romans, then came his brothers, wife and daughter, and last of all Caratacus himself. Totally defeated, bereft of all means of defiance save of courage, he stood proudly before the crowd. While the other prisoners sued for mercy, he declared that Rome's intention to rule the world did not mean that all men should accept servitude! Claudius, who knew what courage meant, magnanimously freed Caratacus and all his family, who thenceforward lived in honourable retirement in Rome.

Britain was not the only province to be added to the Empire during Claudius's reign. Thrace in Greece, Judea in the Near East, and Mauretania in North Africa, were brought under his sway.

At home Claudius proved an able ruler. He subsidised shipowners and shipbuilders to ensure the essential imports of corn for Rome's growing population, and rebuilt the harbour at Ostia, Rome's port, with massive breakwaters and a landing pier. He reorganised Rome's water supply, tapping new sources and constructing new reservoirs. He introduced humane legislation regarding slaves; the killing of sick slaves was now held to be murder. According to Tacitus, he expelled the Jews from Rome because they were filled with unrest 'at the instance of their leader, Chrestus'. Perhaps this means that he persecuted the Christians, his government not distinguishing between the Jews of the Synagogue and the Jews of the Cross; yet he escaped the odium of Christian writers which fell so heavily upon his successor, Nero.

In his private life he was unfortunate. His third wife, Messalina, was little better than a strumpet and her behaviour a public scandal. Claudius not only tolerated her outrageous sexual adventures but was guided by her in many official matters. However, he reached the limit of patience when she went through a marriage ceremony with one of her lovers, and had her executed by the guards, considering, naturally enough, that his own position as Emperor had somehow been cast in doubt by the bigamy of the Empress.

Through all this, his literary work continued. He had at least one play produced, wrote eight volumes of an autobiography, which is unhappily lost, added three new letters to the alphabet (which were soon dropped) and was a devoted student of Greek. After the death of Messalina, he married Agrippina, daughter of his dead brother Germanicus, though she was his niece. She had a son named Nero by her first husband Domitius. By Messalina Claudius had a daughter Octavia, and a son Britannicus, who was later poisoned by Nero. Claudius, like Augustus, thus had a daughter and a stepson. Like Augustus, he arranged for the two to marry, adopting Nero as his son. The young man, now officially a member of the Julian house, took the name Nero Domitius Caesar. Claudius died, aged sixty-four, in AD 54 after a reign of fourteen years. The circumstances of his death were suspicious and it was generally agreed that Agrippina had poisoned him, using a dish of mushrooms, one of his favourite foods, in order to hasten the accession of her son Nero. She withheld news of Claudius's death until all arrangements had been made for Nero's accession.

The new emperor was only seventeen when Claudius died and his reign opened with brilliant promise. His descent from the great Germanicus ensured his popularity. He began to rule with decorum, reorganising the Senate as a purely aristocratic body, and excluding from it the sons of freedmen, whom Claudius had tolerated. He promised that he would model himself upon the great Augustus and went out of his way to be merciful and compassionate. When signing the order for an execution he would curse the day he learned to write, and all Rome loved him. He increased his popularity by reducing taxes and putting on splendid shows in the theatre, in some of which he would himself participate, for he was a talented musician, though perhaps not quite as good a singer as he believed, and a poet. He also had a taste for architecture, which he was able to indulge after a great and destructive fire in Rome. Rumours spread that Nero himself arranged it to make way for a modern and more glorious city. Perhaps to quell these rumours, the story was put about that the fires had been started by the Christians, 'a group who followed a new and malevolent religion', as Suetonius put it. Nero devised hideous tortures for them. Some, in mockery of their faith, were crucified, some soaked in pitch and set on fire to be living torches. Others, more fortunate, were made to face wild beasts in the arena and died more swiftly.

During his reign a major defeat was inflicted upon the Roman armies in Britain. The rapacity of emperors had become notorious. They frequently confiscated the wealth of men who died, leaving the families destitute. To forestall this, rich men began to leave the Emperor part of their estate, which both satisfied his greed and gave him an interest in the proper execution of the will. In Britain, this practice was followed by Prasutugus, King of the Iceni, a nation dwelling in East Anglia. (The road which is today called the Icknield Way is their memorial.) Prasutugus died in AD 61, leaving a widow, Boudicca, and two daughters. She succeeded to the kingdom and the will was read. The Governor, Paulinus, sent a detachment of troops to collect the emperor's legacy; they treated Boudicca not as an allied queen but as a despised native of a conquered country. Moreover the Roman officer in charge also confiscated the wealth of her nobles, thus enflaming all the leaders of her kingdom. They looted her palace and brutally raped her two daughters. When she protested, they flogged her savagely and so made off with the treasure they had looted.

Boudicca summoned her outraged nation to arms and they marched defiantly, men and women together, against the hitherto invincible legions. She captured Colchester, despite the stout resistance of the legionary veterans, who made a last stand in the temple of Claudius. The Iceni stormed the temple, slaughtering every man within.

The Governor was many miles away in Anglesey, and the

nearest legion far from the scene. The Ninth Legion lay in Lincoln under its commander Cerialis, who, on hearing of the disaster, marched south with 2,000 men to relieve, or if too late, to avenge, the city of Colchester. Boudicca and her army advanced north to meet him. The Ninth was cut to pieces and, though Cerialis and the cavalry escaped, could play no further part in the campaign.

The triumphant Boudicca, her appetite for revenge whetted by the abundant blood of the Ninth, turned savagely towards London. This was not a *municipium* (a self-governing city) like Verulamium, nor a *colonia* (a settlement of ex-servicemen) like Colchester, but a busy trading centre where seagoing ships from the Continent could find safe harbourage. By now the terrible news had reached Paulinus. There was no time for his infantry to outdistance Boudicca, but he set them marching and, accompanied only by his cavalry, he rode as fast as horse could gallop and entered his base in London before the Iceni. There he found that the Second Legion, which he had ordered from Gloucester, had failed him, for their commander, dismayed by the fate of the Ninth, had not dared to advance. Paulinus was isolated in an unwalled town with only a handful of cavalry. He decided to withdraw, to retain his army in being, and to unite the Second Legion with his main forces for the final battle. He abandoned London to its fate, in the vivid phrase of Tacitus, losing a city to save a province. Boudicca thus found London defenceless and swept through the town, putting to the sword those who resisted or who had collaborated with the hated Romans. For some she reserved the crueller fates of crucifixion and the stake. She burned down the warehouses, the shops, the private dwellings and public buildings; the spade still uncovers a layer of ash 12-15ft below the peaceful surface of the present streets, the enduring mark of her fury.

Now her armies, with the flush of invincibility upon them, marched northwards to Verulamium (the modern St Albans), a city recently built under Roman guidance, where the citizens suffered the same savage fate as the Londoners. Here again, burnt pottery, ash, blackened brick and scorched plaster are still found under the cornfields. Tacitus recorded that over 70,000 perished in the sacking of the three towns 'by the sword, by the cross and by fire'.

Paulinus had passed through Verulamium on his way north shortly before it fell to Boudicca, and met his infantry somewhere in the Midlands. His force numbered about 10,000, the Second Legion still skulking in the south-west, and Boudicca's army, elated by victory, far outnumbering his own. Paulinus himself selected the battlefield, positioning his troops between two dense woods. To her rear, Boudicca had drawn up her column of carts and heavy wagons into a solid line, as a final redoubt behind which to retreat if need be. The Romans, horse and foot together, charged with great dash, and the Iceni, trapped between the Roman swords and their own barrier of wagons, were overwhelmed and destroyed. Boudicca poisoned herself and all effective resistance to Rome died with her. If her warlike spirit entered some Valhalla, she had a proud escort of thousands of her own fighting men and those legionaries whom she had sent on ahead. The commander of the Second Legion, appalled by the bloody results of his indecision, killed himself with the sword he had failed to draw in defence of his comrades.

Far from this revolt, in Rome, Nero's taste for the arts became obsessive. He travelled to Greece not so much as an emperor but as a playwright, singer and poet, visiting the land where all these arts had first flourished. On his return he entered Rome in the century-old state coach of Augustus, wearing the wreaths he had won for his singing.

His vices are well known. He practiced incest with his sisters, blatantly placing their portraits upon his coins. He murdered his mother, and raped a vestal virgin. He castrated and then 'married' Sporus, treating the unfortunate man in all ways as his spouse. His wife Octavia, of the line of Augustus, was first divorced and then executed; he next married Statilia, after murdering her husband; and finally Poppaea, who at least had the virtue of matching his own depravity.

A revolt in Gaul under Julius Vindex moved him to warlike preparations and a successful campaign was fought, but then there was an armed revolt by Galba who commanded in Spain. Nero panicked, yet remained more concerned with banquets and music than with defending his Empire. Other armies in other provinces rose against him. He alternated hysterically between plans to create a new realm in the east and suicide. His courage failing, he found no one to give him the mercy of death. Finally he left Rome with Phaon, one of his freedmen, to whose villa he fled. Thence his friends tried to persuade him to make good his escape. Even in despair his egotism triumphed. 'When I die' he said 'what a great artist will be lost!' Phaon, who remained outside to gather news, sent him a note: the Senate had declared him a public enemy and he was to be executed according to ancient custom—flogged to death. Terrified, he tried to commit suicide but his nerve failed him. Then he heard the clatter of approaching horses, the troop of cavalry sent to arrest him. He stabbed himself clumsily in the throat and was slowly dying when the cavalry arrived. With him died the last of the Julian house. Something like 100 years had passed since the Battle of Actium and three generations had lived under the principate. All emperors hitherto had been kin by marriage or by blood to Julius Caesar and Augustus. Where now should Rome find someone to maintain the system? There followed (AD 68-9) 'the year of the three emperors'.

The Senate invited Galba, already in his seventies, to take the government, He had lived through all the preceding reigns and, according to Plutarch, had been greeted as a child by Augustus. His career had been distinguished: he had been a protegé of Livia's after Augustus's death; he had obtained high military command and was a strict disciplinarian; he prided himself upon his physical fitness and had once trotted for 20 miles, in full uniform, beside Caligula's coach; he had won victories in Africa and Germany and had been appointed to the governorship of Spain, which he ruled for eight years. It was there that appeals came to him from Vindex to assist in saving mankind from the inhumanities of Nero. He put Spain into a state of readiness and prepared for war, but then news came of the defeat and death of Vindex and Galba's rebellion nearly collapsed. Fresh news followed, however, of Nero's suicide, whereupon—with no dynastic rights—he assumed the name of Caesar, which was thus finally recognised as a title of majesty. He adopted a handsome young aristocrat named Piso who also received the name of Caesar.

In Rome he imposed strict discipline upon the troops. He executed soldiers and citizens alike, and, in his attempts to clean up the corruption and luxury left by Nero, ruled with stark brutality. A mere six months was sufficient time for the army to conclude that he was a tyrant. An officer named Otho led the rebellion and Galba was cut down and slain by a troop of cavalry in the streets of Rome.

Lucius Otho (said by some to be a bastard son of Tiberius) had been born in AD 32 and had become a great favourite with Nero. The two had quarrelled over Poppaea whom Nero had made Otho marry. The wedding had been intended as a purely formal ceremony in order to reserve her for Nero, but Otho had consummated the marriage and Nero, mad with jealousy, had banished him. At first a supporter of Galba, he saw the opportunity for power in the latter's growing unpopularity. It was he who organised the army's revolt, and it was he who had sent the troop of horsemen to ride down Galba. The Senate accepted him as Caesar.

But again civil war came to Rome. Another ambitious commander, Vitellius, decided to make his bid for power. Throughout the Empire the legions declared for him and Otho, not without dignity, made his peace with his friends and killed himself. In Britain, now an integral part of the Empire, the effects of Vitellius's ambition had been felt. The commanding officer of the Twentieth Legion supported him, and there was friction between Trebellius, the Governor, and the garrisons.

Vitellius, finally victorious, was declared Caesar and Emperor by the enthusiastic armies. He immediately faced a problem with the Fourteenth Legion, which had left Britain, for a detachment from it had fought for Otho and had been routed. The main body had not been defeated and their political stability was dubious. Vitellius ordered them back to Britain where they could do no harm.

E

Meanwhile Vespasian, whom we glimpsed in action in Britain, had bided his time and was advancing on Rome as a rival to Vitellius. Now his troops entered the City unopposed, preventing Vitellius's escape to Campania. Vitellius hid in the doorman's lodge at the palace with a watchdog outside and a bed jammed against the door. Vespasian's troops entered and ransacked the deserted palace. Finding Vitellius, they dragged him to the Forum, with a noose round his neck, and killed him with slow and deliberate cruelty, throwing his body into the Tiber. Vespasian was now Emperor by conquest and had won the name of Caesar by force of arms.

He came from the middle-class Flavian family, but on accession took the name of Caesar. His grandfather, who had fought on the side of Pompey in the civil war, left the army after Pompey's death to become a tax collector. His son, Vespasian's father, was a centurion, but later he too became a tax collector, serving in the Near East. Vespasian was born in AD 9, and could remember the last years of Augustus, who died five years later. He was a man who held ceremony in contempt; it is said that he long refused to wear a broad-bordered toga (the mark of a senator) and did so only when his grandmother insisted. He served with the army in Thrace and was promoted military Tribune, then became Quaestor (senior Magistrate) of Crete and Cyrenaica, when lots were drawn for provincial appointments. Back in Rome, he offered himself as a candidate for the office of Aedile but failed to be elected. He stood a second time and was elected a poor sixth on the list of successful candidates. Later he was elected Praetor, Suetonius alleging that he gained this honour by sycophancy to Caligula.

He married Flavia Domitilla, whose father was no more than a clerk in a Quaestor's office. He had two sons, Titus and Domitian, and a daughter Domitilla. His wife and daughter died while he was still young, and he then lived with Cenis, a woman who had once been the mistress of a freedman. He never married her, but was always faithful to her, and they continued to live together even after he became Emperor.

On Caligula's death he was fortunate in gaining the favour

of Claudius through friendship with Narcissus, Claudius's freedman secretary. With the latter's help he obtained command of the Second Legion, which took part in the invasion of Britain under Plautius, and thus gained the opportunity of enhancing his military reputation. After the battle for the Medway crossing at which we have already glanced, Plautius ordered Vespasian westwards into unknown territory, to carry the eagles of Rome to the Britons dwelling between the Thames and the Exe. He led his troops with skill and dash. The long march was through hostile country, past unknown cities and strongholds. Suetonius tells us that he completely conquered two tribes and captured more than twenty *Oppida* or tribal towns. Stiff battles must have been fought for many of these. One was almost certainly the great fortified strongpoint of Maiden Castle, brilliantly excavated by Sir Mortimer Wheeler. It is a vast, seemingly impregnable, stronghold set on a hill surrounded by huge ramparts and ditches. The skeletons of some of the British defenders have been uncovered, their bones still showing the wounds inflicted by Roman swords. In the spine of one is still embedded the iron arrowhead which killed him. The bodies show every sign of hasty burial and Sir Mortimer Wheeler has called the place the first British War Cemetery. Vespasian's troops may also have stormed the forbidding heights of Old Sarum (just outside modern Salisbury), a fortified stronghold on the crest of a steep hill whose sides are as sheer as any cliff, with deep trenches and high earth walls, rendering any assault murderously difficult. He also crossed the Solent, and seized the Isle of Wight. The brilliance of his campaign was recognised. He was decorated with the Triumphal regalia and returned to Rome with his reputation vastly enhanced. The seeds of his greatness had been sown in the island of Britain.

When Claudius died, Vespasian's star had declined, for Nero's mother Agrippina nursed a hatred for all the friends of Narcissus. Nevertheless Vespasian achieved a Consulship, though only nominally, holding it merely for the last month of a year. But this gave him the right to a proconsular post and he was appointed to North Africa. His governorship was

marked by efficiency and justice, and he added civil achievement to his military reputation. Unlike most governors he did
not profit from his appointment, but returned to Rome no
richer than before. Suetonius wrote that, to secure an income
proportionate to his dignity, he went into the business of
hiring out mules. To raise the necessary capital he sold his
property to his brother. The public, amused, nicknamed him
'the mule driver'!

He accompanied Nero on the latter's visit to Greece. Something of a philistine, he failed to hide his impatience with
Nero's boring songs and, during recitals, used to creep out of
the room or nod in his chair and doze. This did not endear him
to the vain and wayward Nero, and for a while he was forced
to withdraw from court circles.

Trouble was now brewing in the East. The Jews were still
looking for their Messiah, for Christ, crucified some thirty
years earlier, had been accepted as the Annointed One only by
a handful of the Judeans. Rumours of the Messiah continued
to spread into the Roman world, taking the form of a prophecy
that out of Judea should come those who would rule the world.
The Jews, exhilarated by the prophecy, rose against the
Romans and killed the Procurator. The Governor of Syria
marched against them, but they defeated him and inflicted the
final disgrace upon his troops by capturing one of the Eagles.
An expeditionary force was organised to re-establish Rome's
reputation. The authorities did not want an ambitious man
who might exploit the wide powers that would have to be
given him, and remembered Vespasian as a modest and effec-
ient commander. He was sent with two legions, eight wings of
cavalry and ten additional units. With him, as a member of
his staff, he took his son Titus. Vespasian was a strict disciplinarian, and restored the morale of the local troops. He
had lost none of his dash in battle, fought alongside his soldiers
in the field, and was wounded in action by a sling shot.

While he was in Judea the civil war between Otho and
Vitellius broke out. The precedent of Galba had established
that a successful commander could become Emperor by force
of arms. Vespasian was quick to realise that there need be no

limit to his ambitions, notwithstanding his humble beginnings,
and that even the name of Caesar was a not impossible prize.

The Romans delighted in recording omens—usually after
the events they presaged. Suetonius does this for Vespasian.
Most of the prophecies appear nonsensical, but one, true or
false, is worth repeating. In Judea he captured a man named
Joseph, one of the Jewish leaders, known to history as
Josephus. Later Josephus made his peace with the Romans and
subsequently fought on their side. He wrote a history of the
Jewish wars and recorded a full account of Vespasian's
campaign. Suetonius writes that Josephus while a prisoner
told Vespasian that he would be set free by the man who had
captured him, and that this man would become emperor.

When the news of Otho's suicide reached the eastern
provinces, an army of 2,000 men was on the march to assist
his cause. Their purpose gone, discipline broke down and they
ran amok in the town of Aquileia, looting and ransacking. The
rioting troops, remembering how Galba the soldier had come
to power, saw no reason why they should not themselves
select a successor. Some had served under Vespasian, whose
bluff fighting qualities they admired. They decided he should
be their emperor and, as a sign of their intentions, inscribed
his name upon their standards. Discipline was reimposed and
nothing came of their action, but the fire they had lit
smouldered throughout the East. The Governor of Egypt
declared for Vespasian and his own troops in Judea acclaimed
him Emperor. The legions in Syria also supported him and he
received formidable reinforcements from the King of Parthia.
Meanwhile Vitellius had seized power in Rome. Vespasian,
whose strength lay in the East, took immediate steps to secure
his base and occupied the port of Alexandria, where news
came to him of Vitellius's death. Then, with the powerful
support of his armies, he travelled to Rome and took his place
as Emperor.

He was faced with two sets of problems, moral and financial.
Army discipline was lax, the people restive, and Rome slipping
fast into moral decay. The treasury was exhausted by a year
of civil war, its resources wasted in many battles.

He tightened up army discipline, making it clear that he despised the sycophancy and luxury that had flourished under the recent Julian Emperors. One unfortunate young officer, who had dressed with great care for an audience with Vespasian to seek promotion, arrived scented and perfumed. Vespasian bluntly told him that he would have been more welcome if he had smelt decently of garlic! He punished the troops who, during the disturbances, had been guilty of excesses, and withheld from some of the more restless units the bounties due to them for victories in the field. By these and other means he let it be seen that the firm hand of a military commander now held the reins.

Dealing with civilian matters, he expelled the unworthy from the ranks of the Senate and the Knights of Rome. He strengthened the two orders by enrolling new members of merit—even from among provincials. He introduced social legislation to check the license of earlier reigns, was at pains to strip his own office of some of the humourless pomp that by now surrounded it, and laughed when flattering historians tried to trace his ancestry back to an aristocratic beginning. He heartily disliked too much ceremony. Most men, when awarded a Triumph revelled in the dazzling ritual, but he found his own Triumph a bore. He told his friends he had never sought the honour, having no distinguished ancestors whose memory he could thus glorify, and never having nursed any personal ambition for a Triumph. He discouraged his friends from striking humble postures and behaving like courtiers. Even the anti-imperial Suetonius can find very little harsh to say against him. Under his guidance the law was justly and fairly administered. The healthy concept that the Princeps was first citizen rather than a demi-god came like a breath of fresh air into the oppressive atmosphere of Rome.

Financially, he was faced with grave difficulties; he estimated that 400 million gold pieces were needed for the country's recovery. He ended the wildly extravagant banquets of earlier Emperors. Nor was he ashamed to trade, buying and selling commodities for profit and thus enhancing his personal fortune, which he used in the service of the state. He increased taxes in the provinces and missed no chance of raising money. Before his day the public lavatories in Rome were free, their cost being met by the sale of ammonia to the bleaching industry. He imposed a charge of a copper, much to the disgust of his son Titus. His reply to his son's criticism was to the point; he passed a coin to him and asked, 'Does it smell?' When Titus agreed that it did not, Vespasian's rejoinder was, 'That's strange, it comes from one of the public lavatories!' (To this day, Italians call a public lavatory a *vespasiano*.) Immortality can come to a man in a strange guise!

He did not confound meanness with economy, however. So that senators could maintain their rank, he subsidised the poorer senatorial families and awarded pensions to ex-consuls. Although he had been bored by Nero's concerts, he gave grants to actors and musicians and also to teachers.

His coin portraits show a tough, rugged face with a jutting jaw and tightly pursed lips. To compare his coins with those of his aristocratic predecessors is to glimpse the contrast between his conception of his office and theirs. From Augustus to Nero, all have the fine features of aristocrats. His own nose is hooked, his eyes small, and his expression grim. It was jokingly said that he always looked constipated, and the coins give point to the story. He had an irrepressible sense of humour, much of which was directed against himself. Once a woman at court wheedled 4,000 gold pieces out of him on the pretext that she loved him. When his secretary asked how this should be entered in the books, he said, 'Oh, put it down as expenses—for a passion for Vespasian!'

Vespasian made a brilliant appointment in Britain, sending Agricola as Governor, under whose administration the final conquest was achieved, the island explored, and the process of Romanisation accelerated. When Agricola arrived in the summer of AD 78 the Britons were growing restive. Just before they had attacked and destroyed a wing of cavalry on one of the frontiers and there were signs of further risings. Although the campaigning season was almost over, Agricola marched westwards against them, then swung north and occupied the Isle of Anglesey.

Having shown his military might, he began to reform the civil administration, bringing a liberal mind to the problem of transforming a conquered people into willing allies. He pardoned minor faults but was strict about great ones; nor did he punish where he could win contrition. He relieved the Britons of some of the more onerous taxes. Within a year, this liberal policy had wrought dramatic changes and he was able to spend the following summer leading his army on a tour of exploration rather than of warfare.

In the third year he marched north to the Firth of Tay, into lands that had not yet seen the might of Rome. Each succeeding summer he went on campaign and had he remained long enough might well have conquered what is now Scotland. In one of his campaigns he fought a pitched battle against the Caledonians who, after their cavalry was defeated, took to the hills and waged a guerilla war. The Romans were vastly outnumbered but Agricola brought his forces back to safety through the wild mountains and narrow glens.

Unusually for a Roman commander, he also made use of a fleet to learn about the country. He organised a combined operation, with the fleet exploring the coastline and harbours, while the infantry marched along the shore, maintaining close contact with the ships, showing the power of Rome to many distant tribes.

He struck a careful balance between military operations and the peaceful development of the province. He provided a liberal education for the sons of local kings and chieftains, so that a generation of native rulers would grow up in sympathy with the aims and culture of Rome. It was during his day that the toga was introduced into the island. Porticoes and public baths were built. Latin began to be spoken, at any rate by the nobles of each tribe. The mining and metal-refining industries were organised under government control and ingots stamped with Agricola's name have been found. In St Albans fragments of inscribed stone dating from the time of his governorship have been discovered. The style of the lettering indicates that they were carved by an Italian craftsman, suggesting that Agricola brought not only soldiers but workmen to the island.

Judging by the size of the inscription the fragments come from a very large public building, and show how the old tribal city was being transformed into the luxurious Roman city of Verulamium.

Agricola's appointment has indirectly given us detailed knowledge of Roman Britain up to his day, since his son-in-law Cornelius Tacitus was one of his greatest admirers. Tacitus was an outstanding historian and the most distinguished prose writer of the age. Because of his deep admiration for his father-in-law he wrote the latter's biography, which contains a succinct narrative of events in Britain from the Claudian invasion to Agricola's own appointment. Tacitus describes not merely events but the national character and military methods of the Britons, and it is to his pages that we owe much of our knowledge.

Vespasian died as he had lived, humorously. Smitten with diarrhoea, he struggled to rise, saying that an emperor ought to die on his feet. On his death in AD 79 the succession passed smoothly to his son Titus, whose reign lasted only two years. Like his father, he had built the foundation of his military reputation in Britain, as well as in Germany. While he was Emperor numerous statues of him were set up in both countries. A new generation had grown up in the island since the conquest, and resentment was giving place to pride in the links with Rome. That two Caesars had started their careers in Britain, had brought a new glory to the province and the statues of Titus were visible expressions of this pride.

One of the most notable events of his reign occurred in AD 79 when the city of Pompeii was destroyed by an eruption of Vesuvius. This disaster, in which the elder Pliny perished, has given us a complete Roman city, with the houses and shops, and the bodies of its citizens preserved in lava, just as they were when ruin overtook them.

Titus died peaceably in bed at the age of forty-two in AD 81. Some said his early death was due to the curse he had incurred by entering the Holy of Holies in the Temple of Jerusalem, which he had captured during his father's reign. He was universally mourned by common people and Senate alike. His had been a quiet and decent reign, based on a sound and just administration, with pleasant dinner parties rather than ostentatious banquets, and with a return to the ancient virtues. It had been marred by only one thing—the plots of his younger brother Domitian against him.

Domitian succeeded to the Empire in AD 81 and ruled very differently from his father and brother: he used his power capriciously and Rome lost the decorum and stability it had begun to acquire. Back came the extravagance and depravity that Vespasian and Titus had banished, and back came an irresponsible cruelty that reminds us of the worst days of Tiberius or Caligula.

He recalled Agricola from Britain, prematurely as Tacitus alleges. The charge was perhaps unfair, for Agricola had enjoyed seven years as Governor and had had time to fight numerous campaigns, as we have seen. But Tacitus suggests that Domitian was jealous of Agricola's achievements, which he could not but contrast with his own recent pseudo-Triumph over the Germans, in which not prisoners but slaves disguised as Germans had followed his chariot.

His tyranny evoked considerable opposition, to which he reacted with fear and violence. He executed his opponents without compunction until, after fifteen years of misrule, he was assassinated in September AD 96. The plot against him, which was triggered off by his execution upon some groundless charge of a cousin of his, Flavius Clemens, was headed by his wife Domitia and by the Prefect of the Praetorian Guard. He had for many days been filled with forebodings that his death was near. His assassins played on this and gained access to him by claiming that they were able to reveal a plot against his life; then they stabbed him and he died in terror, calling vainly for a dagger to defend himself.

After his death his name was erased from the records and expunged from many monuments, including the stone from St Albans, bearing Agricola's name, mentioned above.

The Flavian Dynasty was now extinct. To succeed Domitian, the Senate chose Marcus Cocceius Nerva, a man of sixty-four, bestowing upon him the name of Caesar and the title of

Augustus. He had no military claims to office, being a lawyer rather than a soldier, but had twice held the Consulship, once with Vespasian and once with Domitian. His brief two-year reign marked a return to decency and tranquillity. The cruelty of Domitian became no more than an evil memory. Nerva had restored the dignity of the Senate and the liberties of the people by the time of his death in AD 98 and with his death the first century drew towards a close. It had seen the end of the house of Julius Caesar and Augustus, had firmly established the rule of one sole emperor, and had turned the family name of Caesar into a title of authority and a designation of supreme power.

III · TRAJAN TO SEVERVS

The Empire at its Height - Second Century AD

The second century was at first a period of great Emperors. Trajan, Hadrian, Antoninus Pius and Marcus Aurelius were outstanding men and under them the Empire achieved its peak of stability and prosperity. Later there was a falling away from their high standards, and the chill shadow of decline began to be felt.

A year before he died Nerva looked round for a successor. He was the first Emperor since Nero who had not been a soldier, and he knew that the experiment had not been an unqualified success. Despite the wisdom and justice of his reign, he had never enjoyed more than formal support from the army. Affection they withheld. Accordingly he looked for an heir among the leading soldiers of the day, and selected a Spaniard named Marcus Ulpius Trajanus, who had seen distinguished service. He had been born at Italica, near Seville, and was forty-five years old. Trajan had enlisted when quite young, and had served near the Euphrates when he was twenty-eight, seeing action against the Parthians in the Near East. Later he entered the civil magistracy, becoming Praetor some time before his thirty-fourth birthday and Consul when he was thirty-nine. Then, after a spell back home in Spain, he rejoined the army and was appointed by Domitian to command the troops in lower Germany.

By now it had become standard practice for the Emperor to adopt his heir, and, having taken his decision, the ageing Nerva accordingly adopted Trajan as his son. The Spanish officer thus received the name of Caesar and succeeded peacefully to the Principate when Nerva died in AD 98.

The stability which the Empire had acquired under Vespasian and his successors was dramatically illustrated. Trajan, who was at Cologne when the news of Nerva's death reached him, had no reason to fear that Rome would again witness scenes like those that had followed the death of Caligula. He made no haste to return to the capital to secure his position. Content to leave affairs at Rome in the hands of the Senate, he first completed his work on the Rhine and then launched a new campaign on the Danube frontier. Perhaps because of his early experience, his military interests lay largely in the East. He twice fought campaigns in Dacia (southwestern Russia), first in 101 and again in 104.

After the second campaign he celebrated a Triumph and the public games in Rome lasted for seven weeks; 10,000 Dacian prisoners died in the arena and 11,000 wild animals were butchered, reminding us that at the heart of Roman society there lay a savage and unquenchable thirst for blood. More enduring than the tumultuous glory of this Triumph was the memorial Trajan erected in 112—an immense stone column, which stands in Rome to this day. Around it winds a long strip of carvings in bold relief depicting Trajan's campaigns with extraordinary vividness. We can watch (as precisely as if the scenes had been photographed) his troops on the march, fighting, and sailing in their ships; we can see the towns he assaulted and the vanquished barbarians falling under the hooves of his heavy armoured cavalry.

In 114 he led another expedition eastwards, into Parthia. Having crossed the Tigris, he and his legions entered Babylon and Ctesiphon; and in 116 he stood on a sandy shore looking

out over the blue waters of the Persian Gulf. No Roman
Emperor had marched so far before. The legions had sweated
their long way, pack on back, with bronze helmets and equipment hot to the touch in the thirsty sunshine, for over 1,000
miles, rivalling the achievements of the armies of Alexander.
Dio tells us that in one of the harbours Trajan saw a ship
bound for India. He told his friends that had he been younger
he would have gone aboard. How different the world's history
might have been had he and his legions sailed for the conquest
of India.

During Trajan's nineteen years' reign, no dramatic events
in Britain are recorded. Some pottery of the Trajan period is
to be found in Scotland, but troops were withdrawn from the
Caledonian outposts and a frontier was drawn up between
north and south Britain. North of the frontier lay the wild
and mountainous land of Caledonia, which remained for ever
unsubdued.

South of the frontier, in Roman Britain proper, the Roman
system of government prevailed. The highest rank a provincial
city could enjoy was to be a *municipium* (municipality) and
in Britain only Verulamium (St Albans) achieved this rank.
In the great basilicon built there by Agricola sat the local
equivalent of the Senate, known as the *Ordo*, presided over by
two magistrates who were the provincial equivalent of the
consuls. In addition there were two other magistrates, who,
like the aediles in Rome, looked after the town's public buildings and physical amenities. The basilicon was a vast building
some 400ft long and 200ft wide, housing not only the council
chamber but the municipality's administrative staff and other
officials. The whole city had been rebuilt after Boudicca's
sacking of the old town.

This form of administration was not unique to the *municipia*
and many other cities in Britain and the other provinces
enjoyed similar forms of local government. In some cases no
doubt the descendants of the former kings and nobles sat in
the assemblies and were appointed to the magistracies.
Agricola's policy of providing a liberal education for the sons
of local princes was now bearing fruit, for by the time of

Trajan the generation Agricola had trained was grown to manhood. They sat in the pillared halls of the local assemblies, proudly wearing their togas, speaking Latin, and accepting the new form of government, which had replaced the old monarchical system but had not diminished their personal glory.

Other towns in the provinces held the rank of *coloniae* These were not colonies in our sense of the word but settlements of time-expired legionaries, who owned and worked the nearby farms, whose size depended upon their rank and years of service. Each *colonia* thus provided a reserve of seasoned troops, still of an age capable of bearing arms, swiftly available in times of trouble. There were four such in Britain: Colchester (Camulodunum), the oldest, dating from the time of Claudius; Lincoln (Lindum Colonia), the name of which city still echoes its former standing; York (Eboracum), the great military centre of the north; and Gloucester (Glevum). Around Lincoln many of the fields are still rectangular and the hedgerows follow the outlines of the vanished farms laid out with military precision for the time-expired soldiers. Like the *municipiae*, the *coloniae* had their psuedo-Senate and their magistrates. To give a focus for the citizens' loyalty to Rome, both had their priests of Augustus, who maintained the cult of emperor worship.

The important town of London was surprisingly neither a *municipium* nor a *colonia*. It was, as now, a busy commercial centre and possibly the financial capital. Wooden writing tablets that have been recovered are branded with the stamp of the Procurator of Britain, the chief financial official of the province.

Many of the Romanised towns were developments of pre-Roman cities and took their names from the nations who had originally built them: near Silchester are still to be seen the gaunt walls of *Calleva Atrebatum*, Calleva of the Atrebates, which was the nation dwelling in the old kingdom of Commius; Winchester was *Venta Belgarum*, the town of the Belgae; and Caistor-next-Norwich was once *Venta Icenorum*, the town of Boudicca's nation, the Iceni. Rome modified but did not reject the tribal divisions she had found in Britain and other provinces. Paris and Amiens echo the names of vanished nations. In the countryside round each of the larger towns still dwelt members of the original tribes. Living in the farmhouses and villages they still looked upon the local town as their capital. Each town, with its dependent lands, was called a *civitas*, or state. Perhaps Rome's own origins, in a group of tribes, helped to make her sensitive and constructive in Britain and the other provinces.

We can still trace through their modern names many of the towns the Romans built in Britain. Later, when the Saxons came to the island, they thought of all Romans as soldiers, and of all their towns as military camps. The Latin for camp was *castra*, which on Saxon tongues became Chester, Cester or some other variant: so Manchester, Leicester, Exeter, Dorchester, Cirencester, Godmanchester are all the modern successors of Roman towns. The true military centres were Richborough, where a great harbour had been built at the place where Aulus Plautius had landed, and from which a road ran straight and true to London; Caerleon-on-Usk, where lay the Second Legion, the unit once commanded by Vespasian; York, from which the northern frontier with Caledonia could be guarded; and Chester, the home of the Twentieth Legion, nicknamed The Victorious, which originally guarded the province from the incursions of the unsubdued nations living in the mountains of northern Wales, and which later looked watchfully towards the Irish Sea. To this day the streets of Chester follow the alignment of the paths of a Roman legionary camp; at the intersection of these pathways once stood the legion's headquarters and upon that spot now stands the town hall.

The legions in Britain were stationed permanently in the island. Once a man had enlisted there was no home leave, for his posting, like the location of the legions, was permanent. In the days of Claudius only citizens could serve, but later on provincials could enlist and Roman citizenship was one of the rewards granted to a veteran. Another was the right to contract a legal marriage: while serving, the men could establish relationships with women only on the basis of concubinage but after honourable discharge they could legalise these unions and legitimise their children. Documents of discharge, engraved on lead so that men might treasure them and leave them to their children, have been dug up in Britain. These documents (*diplomas*) show the name of the unit in which a man served, his rank, and the number of years he had soldiered. Many ex-servicemen from all parts of the Empire were given land in the *coloniae*. Consequently, the population became mixed, as retired legionaries from Gaul, Italy, Thrace, Yugoslavia and elsewhere married and settled in the island. The new Britons, of increasingly mixed descent, more and more identified themselves with the Mediterranean culture of which they were politically, and increasingly ethnically, a part.

Trajan had a kinsman, Publius Aelius Hadrianus, who was born in AD 76 in Italica, Trajan's own Spanish birthplace. At the age of ten he was orphaned and Trajan became one of his guardians. The other was Asilius Attianus, later colonel of the Praetorian Guard and always a faithful supporter of Hadrian. No one then foresaw the imperial glory that was to come to Trajan and through him to Hadrian, who was a studious boy, so devoted to Greek literature that he was nicknamed 'the little Greek'. Much of his youth was spent in Italy. When he was fifteen he returned to Spain and was enrolled in the army. After his initial military service he was given the next step forward in the *Cursus Honorum* and was given a junior magistracy in Rome. Later he was promoted Tribune of the Second Legion, nicknamed the Adjutrix or 'Auxiliary'. This legion (not to be confused with the regular Second Legion— Augusta) had been formed by Vespasian and had included an auxiliary force of marines. When Nerva succeeded Domitian and adopted Trajan as his heir, Hadrian was serving in Moesia (modern Bulgaria). Then, on learning of Nerva's death in AD 97, Hadrian was the first to carry the news to Trajan, though his enemies tried to prevent him. Thenceforward he became one of Trajan's closest friends and later married the latter's niece. Some say that Trajan himself was

F

not anxious for the match and that it was largely arranged by his wife Plotina.

Hadrian was still not Trajan's adopted son, but merely his one-time ward. Though not yet acknowledged as Trajan's heir, he occasionally acted as the Emperor's deputy. Once, when he read a message from Trajan to the Senate, the grave senators chuckled at his outlandish Latin, marred as it was by a heavy Spanish accent. He accompanied Trajan in the first Dacian war without any official appointment but as a friend. The two became drinking companions and spent many a merry evening with the cares of office cast aside and the wine-cups passing. During the second Dacian war, when he was about thirty, he was given command of the First Legion; he carried out his duties with distinction and Trajan significantly rewarded him with a diamond which he himself had been given by Nerva. He was then appointed Governor of Pannonia (approximately the modern Austria). On his return to Rome, he was given the rank of Consul and was appointed Governor of Syria in 117.

In that year Trajan, having watered his cavalry in the Tigris, and having stood on the shore of the Persian Gulf, marched northwards for the conquest of all Arabia. At the siege of Atra he fell ill. A sick man, he was taken westwards into Cilicia (southern Turkey), where he died in the nineteenth year of his reign.

Hadrian, in Syria, was not far away. According to his biographer (Aelius Spartianus) he was told on 9 August that he had been formally adopted by Trajan as the latter's son, thus achieving the name of Caesar and the right of succession. Two days later he heard of Trajan's death and always celebrated that date as the anniversary of his accession as Emperor. The circumstances were mysterious and indeed suspicious. The two men had long been intimates and Trajan could have made a formal act of adoption much earlier, had he so intended. As it was, the news of the old Emperor's death followed a little too pat upon the news of Hadrian's belated adoption. Indeed, many said that Trajan had in fact nominated a man named Priscus to be his heir and that the events of 9 and 11

August had been contrived by Plotina. Whatever the truth may have been, Hadrian felt secure enough not to hasten back to Rome. As Governor of Syria his headquarters were at Antioch, and he stayed there long enough to negotiate a settlement with the Parthians and to take other measures in the East. Only then did he travel to Cilicia to pay his respects to Trajan's ashes; these were then taken in state to Rome, so that the dust of the world's ruler might rest in the capital of the world.

Forty years old, with many years' experience both as military commander and provincial governor. Hadrian came to power at a time when there was a growing restiveness in many of the provinces. He dropped the expansionist policy of Trajan and returned to the more cautious doctrine of Augustus, seeking to consolidate the Empire within its natural boundaries; accordingly, he gave up all the lands that Trajan had conquered between the Euphrates and the Tigris. Rome's future wars with Persia cast some doubts upon the wisdom of this action.

Hadrian was not merely one of the best but one of the most popular of the emperors. He had all the good sense and humour of Vespasian with a vastly more handsome and commanding presence, and the fortunate Empire he inherited did not require the unpopular economies that Vespasian had been compelled to make. His wisdom, moderation and justice brought him the acclaim of the army and the affection of the people. During the first few years of his reign, apart from a visit to the Danube, he spent his time in Rome. Then, in 120 or 121 he set out on a tour of Germany and Britain.

At that time Spartianus records that 'for some time it had not been possible to hold the Britons under the jurisdiction of Rome'. We do not know what risings against the Roman garrisons lay behind these words, but from what followed we may guess that the Caledonians in the north, encouraged by Trajan's withdrawal of Rome's forces from their heathered hills, had struck deep into those regions which are now Cumberland, Durham and Yorkshire. These troubles may have

been graver than mere unrest, for about this time the Ninth
Legion vanished from the scene. This was the unit which
under the leadership of Cerialis had played such a gallant part
in the war with Boudicca. In what disaster it perished no one
now knows. Almost certainly it was overrun by a raid in force
from the north. Maybe it suffered not only defeat but disgrace,
for although other legions, when severely reduced by heavy
casualties, had been re-formed with drafts of new recruits,
the Ninth disappeared from the Army List and was never
heard of again. Its successor in Britain was the Sixth
Legion.

So five years after his accession, in 122, Hadrian came to
Britain, the fifth Caesar to do so, but unlike his predecessors
he came not to conquer but to defend. The visit was also part
of his general policy of seeing for himself; for he was the first
Emperor to visit every province of the Empire. On these
journeys, he did not travel in state but marched as a soldier
among his troops, walking bareheaded in all weathers, eating
the ordinary camp rations of bread and cheese, bacon and
sour wine. He wore no imperial robes but a standard uniform
with plain unjewelled swordbelt. The only sign of his majesty
was a modest ivory hilt to his sword. He personally inspected
the camps and garrisons, throwing out the luxurious furniture
and fittings with which military stations were now beginning
to be cluttered, to the detriment of discipline. He marched
his 20 miles a day with the legions, visited sick soldiers in
their quarters, inspected the forts and strong points, and
examined the rolls of enlisted men, discharging all those over
age. (There was a growing tendency for soldiers to stay on
for the sake of the pay and rations when they were long past
fighting age.) He also stopped the promotion of mere boys
from rich families to sinecures on the staff of legionary commanders.

His travels in Britain and elsewhere became famous in
Rome. It was also a matter for amused gossip that he, the emperor of the world, was content to march round on foot. One
of his friends, Florus the poet wrote a jingle and sent it to him:

> I would hate to be poor Caesar
> Walking round among the Britons,
> Sitting idly in the cookshops . . .
> Putting up with Scythian winters.

Hadrian, not to be outdone, wrote a jingle in reply:

> I would hate to be poor Florus
> Walking round among the taverns,
> Sitting idly in the cookshops . . .
> Putting up with fat round bugs there.

Wherever he went, he looked into grievances and relieved the citizens of unfair taxes. There is interesting archaeological evidence for the dishonest practices of some tax collectors in Britain in a fine bronze corn measure stamped with the Emperor's name and clearly designed for official use. Taxes on land were in kind, and the tax collectors went from farm to farm at harvest time to take the corn that was due. This particular measure, however, took more than its due, being about 15 per cent oversize—the 15 per cent becoming the tax collector's perquisite!

The Britons, whose towns were now miniature replicas of the fabled City of Rome, must have gazed with awe at the sturdy bearded figure of Hadrian. For all the simplicity of his dress he was the Augustus, ruler of the world, the godlike man whom they were led to worship by their priests, the *Augustales*. He had come among them, to walk bareheaded through the rain and mist of their own country, visiting the basilica, consulting the local magistrates, inspecting the tax collectors' records and setting right so much that was wrong. His presence, and his intervention in their affairs, bound them closer than ever before to the glories of Rome.

More lasting than the imperial memories of his visit was the vast frontier work he built to divide Roman Britain from the unconquered lands of Caledonia. The immensity of the work suggests that Trajan's withdrawal of the garrisons and outposts from the hills and glens of the north had produced bitter fruit. The untamed Picts and Caledonians, now secure from the threat of Roman troops in their midst, moved over to the offensive. They had to be conquered or contained. Hadrian's solution was to fortify the frontier rather than to embark on a costly and bloody campaign, and his Wall remains one of the wonders of the ancient world. When new, with the grey masonry and bonding courses of red brick still bright in the northern sunshine, the turned earth of the defensive ditch still fragrant in the border rain, it was a vivid reminder of Rome's task of keeping the envious barbarians at bay. To the south, the roads of Britain linked the old tribal capitals with one another, and stretched purposefully to the great ports of the south coast. Thence laden ships crossed the Channel to Gaul, whence other roads ran to each province and to the Eternal City itself. But north of the Wall there was only the tangle of gorse and heather, intersected by mere tracks. There the Picts and Caledonians still retained their tribal society, as they had for generations. Coming into the Roman province for trade, and sometimes to serve in the Roman army, they had seen the treasures and luxuries of the warm villas. In the market places they had seen the good Roman money of gold, silver and bronze, all to be secured for the price of a brisk battle.

The Wall stretches some 73 Roman miles from the Tyne Estuary to the Solway. The remaining sections, marching across wide moorland and commanding the countryside to the north, still speak eloquently of the immensity of Hadrian's conception. The survey alone, across territory that was largely hostile, must have been a massive task. The Wall's right flank lay on the north bank of the Tyne, some $4\frac{1}{2}$ miles from the sea. It cut across a loop of that river, touching it again about $3\frac{1}{4}$ miles to the south-west. At this point a bridge called Pons Aelius (one of Hadrian's names) reminds us of the designer. Thence it ran with an occasional change of direction, to another bridge over the Tyne some 25 miles from the sea. Here a large fort, whose remains are still to be seen, protected the river crossing. It then climbed a steep slope, rising some 300ft in less than a mile, to the top of Teppermoor Hill, whence it swung south to the peaks of Carrawbrough and

Carrow, striding south-west across high land for a further 10 miles. Much of this section still stands, majestic even today. It then followed the lower contours, leaving the peaks to the south, to cross the River Irthing. Here, after another change of direction, the Wall followed a long ridge southwestwards, with the river lying to the south behind the uplands. It strode down from the ridge to cross two more streams and so south-west by south to the lower lands lying north of the River Eden. Here there was a bridge and the Wall struck north-west again, skirting an area of salt marshes and the low southern shore of the Solway Firth, until it reached Bowness-on-Solway, where its western flank was protected by a great fort.

In Germany, Hadrian had seen parts of the frontier protected by timber palisades. On the windswept moors of northern Britain, however, timber was scarce but stone abundant, as was limestone with which to make cement. So the Wall in Britain, unlike its counterparts in Germany, was built of masonry. Close to it there are still to be seen the scars in the hillsides from which the legionaries quarried the stone which went into the building. The Wall had a rubble and mortar core, which was faced with neatly squared stone. Along the facing there were horizontal courses of red brick to provide a firm bond.

The quarrying, dressing and transporting of the stone, the calcining of the limestone, and the labour of building occupied many men for a long period. Hadrian could not have personally supervised the construction, for his visit was too brief. Nothing more than the preliminary survey could have been completed under his direction, and the main work was carried out by Platorius, the Governor whose name is recorded in inscriptions. The Roman legionary was extraordinarily versatile. An invincible infantryman, he could build an overnight camp or a permanent fortress, construct a bridge or lay a road. Individual military units were responsible for stretches of 30 to 40ft of the Wall, and each unit set up a stone inscribed with the number of its legion or cohort, and sometimes with the name of its officer, at the end of its section.

Among the units there was a detachment of the *Classis Britannica*—the British fleet.

At intervals of about a mile there were small strongpoints known as milecastles. Each contained a small guard and each could communicate with the others through smaller signal turrets set up between them. There were also much larger forts, one on each flank and others at irregular intervals along the Wall. In the rear there were barracks for large numbers of troops, with stables and bath houses. Some 40,000 troops were probably required to man the whole defence system of the Wall.

The Wall was completed about 127 and performed its function effectively until the end of the second century, when large stretches were pulled down in the course of a Caledonian invasion. It was rebuilt by Severus and was garrisoned until about 385, when it was finally overrun. The last details we have of the garrison are recorded in the *Notitia Dignitatum*, the fifth-century list of the civil and military establishments of the Empire, which recorded the units manning the Wall in case it was ever recovered. There was a cohort of soldiers from Dacia, and a unit from a naval squadron, each known as the 'First Aelius', their name commemorating Hadrian. There were cohorts from Gaul, Spain and Thrace and two from the nation of the Nervii (whom Julius Caesar had conquered centuries before). There were Moors, and Helvetii, and men from many other lands, twenty-three individual units being named. So Spaniards and Swiss, Africans and Dacians, stood guard in the chill winters and pale summers of Rome's northern frontier.

There can be little doubt that the idea of a northern wall was conceived by Hadrian himself. Spartianus tells us that he set up defensive works along many of the frontiers. With all western Europe now moving towards civilisation, Hadrian saw the legions as a frontier force and not as armies of occupation. He was not merely the titular head of the Empire, but its active ruler. Because of his wide travels, he knew each province's affairs and problems at first hand. It was said that he understood the finances and economics of all the Roman lands as intimately as a man understands his own household accounts.

Hadrian adopted as his heir a handsome young man named Lucius Ceionius Commodus, who died shortly after the adoption. Hadrian, in the first shock of sorrowful despair, said to his friends 'I have leaned upon a crumbling wall . . .' If the story is true, it shows how deeply the conception of a wall was implanted on his mind as a symbol of security.

Some time during Hadrian's reign there was a disastrous fire in London, and the citizens were faced with the task of replanning their city, which had been rebuilt a mere sixty years earlier after its destruction by Boudicca. It may have been now that the defensive wall was built round the town to the north, east and west. To the south the broad Thames was a sufficient defence. The eastern section of the wall began where the Tower of London now stands, and ran north, where part of it is still to be seen today. At Aldgate it turned north-west towards Cripplegate, where a large bastion (revealed by the bombing in the 1940s) marked the end of the northern defences. It then ran south to Aldersgate, east for a short way, and south again past Ludgate, and so back to the river. It enclosed some 326 acres and its line is still effectively the City's boundary.

There was at least one large bronze statue of Hadrian set up in Britain. A replica has been placed in a little garden among the crowded buildings north of the Tower of London, by the grey stones of a surviving section of the Roman wall.

No great military campaigns marked Hadrian's reign, and his travels through the Empire were made in peace. He saw Athens; and the tower he built there, dedicated to the four winds, stands to this day. He climbed Mt Etna. He saw the dark pine-scented forests of Germany, the sunny olive groves of Spain and the rustling palm trees of Egypt. It was there, on the Nile, that he sustained a deep personal sorrow. He had fallen in love with a handsome young man named Antinous (who came from Bithynia, the scene of Julius Caesar's adventure 200 years before) who survives in many statues. He was Hadrian's companion on many journeys, and was drowned, when they were in Egypt together, in mysterious circumstances. It was said (the story is recorded by Dio) that in Egypt it had been prophesied that death would strike the Emperor's party: and rather than allow the prophecy to be fulfilled by the death of his beloved Hadrian, Antinous drowned himself in the Nile. When he died, Hadrian is said to have wept like a woman. His grief and emotional involvement must have been intense, for the character that emerges from the pages of Spartianus is that of a robust and sturdy man, normally gay and with a great sense of fun. To commemorate his friend, Hadrian named a city after him and issued silver coins bearing his portrait.

Hadrian's biographer tells us several anecdotes to show his ready wit. Once he refused some favour to a grey and elderly suppliant, but the man came back some time later with his hair dyed and renewed his suit. 'Oh', said Hadrian, 'I've already said no to your father!' One of his secret agents intercepted a letter that his wife, Sabina, had sent to one of her lovers, which he read and sent on to her. In it she complained that this man often came to her languid from the luxury of the baths, and useless for the task of love. The next time Hadrian met the man, he read him a lecture (without referring to the letter) on the dangerously enervating effects of the bath.

Like Julius Caesar and Claudius he was author as well as Emperor. He wrote an autobiography (unfortunately lost) and delighted in disputing with scholars and philosophers. When he visited the library at Alexandria, he entered into a lively discussion with the learned men there, asking questions and himself providing the answers. At work he had immense powers of concentration, being able to dictate, read and chat with his friends, all at the same time.

Having, as we have seen, been disappointed in his first choice of an heir by the death of Lucius Ceionius Commodus, he looked round for another successor. This time he selected a brilliant aristocrat named Antoninus, a man of fifty-two, a proven administrator who had for long held a place in his inner councils. Hadrian, in adopting him, made it a condition that Antoninus should adopt the two sons of the dead Commodus so that the seed of his first heir should one day inherit the throne of the Caesars.

Towards the end of his long reign, Hadrian's character changed dramatically—from a hyperactive, gay and robust personality into a figure of gloom and despair. The faithful Antoninus supported him in those dark hours, and it was upon his strong arm that Hadrian leaned when he walked with increasing frailty into the Senate. It was Antoninus who, as Hadrian became more and more depressed, stood between the senators and the old Emperor's unreasoned wrath: he who had always been so just and kindly now condemned men to death capriciously, as if seeking to drown his own despair in the greater despair of others. Towards the end Hadrian lay alone in his villa like a sick lion, broodingly resentful of the unaccustomed weakness that now slackened his muscles. He had always been active, hunting regularly, travelling tirelessly, and exercising with sword and spear. Desperate at finding no cure for his pain and languor, he ordered one of his slaves to run him through with his sword. The man refused. The news was carried to Antoninus, who hastened to the Emperor and tried to comfort the dying man.

After further vain attempts to end his life, Hadrian was taken to Baiae, the seaside resort near Rome, leaving Antoninus in the capital as his deputy. He recovered sufficiently to send for Antoninus but died before the latter could reach him. Sometime before his death he wrote four lines of verse of which any poet might have been proud:

> My little soul, so swift, so sweet,
> My body's guest, my body's friend—
> Soon you will find this fair retreat
> Pale, stiff and naked in the end!
> And no more laughter shall you give
> To flesh when it has ceased to live!

Antoninus succeeded to the Empire with no opposition and no rival, a mature man, only eleven years younger than Hadrian. By now the adoption of a 'son' by an Emperor was simply a means of nominating an heir and of ensuring, by a legal fiction, that the heir bore the magical name of Caesar; but Antoninus, during the sad years of Hadrian's physical and mental decay, had been truly a son to him. He gave to the dead Hadrian's memory the same affectionate consideration. The Senate, forgetting all Hadrian's tireless good works and remembering only his cruelty during his last illness and depression, denied him the divine honours normally paid to dead emperors. But Antoninus brushed their objections aside, and Hadrian, more deserving than many of his predecessors, duly became a god. For his filial piety Antoninus was given the name of Pius—the dutiful.

He had long served the state, having been appointed Consul at the age of thirty-four, and later becoming Proconsul of Asia. where his rule was distinguished for its wisdom and virtue. Thus when Hadrian adopted him in February 138 he was already widely known as a great and good man. On Hadrian's death in July of the same year he fulfilled the dead Emperor's wishes and adopted the two sons of the dead Lucius—Marcus Aurelius Verus and Lucius Aurelius Verus—bestowing upon them the name of Caesar. He did so despite the fact that he was happily married to Faustina, and that his adoption of the two young men removed from the succession any sons that he himself might have. In fact Faustina later bore him two sons, but he remained true to his promise and Marcus Aurelius Verus became his heir.

Antoninus Pius ruled the Empire for twenty-two years, and the history of his reign is almost a complete blank. At home there was no tyranny for the historians to record, and abroad no wars. The tale is one of quiet moderation, with the Empire achieving its highest level of prosperity, and with the peoples of Europe enjoying an unprecedented degree of tranquillity and happiness.

In Britain the most important event during his reign was the building of a further defence work some 75 miles north of Hadrian's Wall. This, known as the Antonine Wall, stretched between the Firth of Forth and the Firth of Clyde, a distance of only 37 miles. It was much slighter than Hadrian's Wall, built of turf and not of stone, with no milecastles and no turrets. There were about a score of forts, but no defence in depth and no large camps to the rear. It was more economical to man than Hadrian's Wall, the total garrison probably being about 7,000 men, but the earlier wall continued to be garrisoned. Perhaps the lowland tribes, through trade, had increasingly come under the influence of Rome. Since the massive masonry of Hadrian's Wall stood between them and the province, their old freebooting life had been destroyed, and they may have turned to their former enemies for protection and for an orderly environment. If this was so, the new turf wall would have been a logical development, protecting the lowland tribes against raids from the sparsely inhabited highlands, and making the lowlands a twilight country between the sunshine of Roman civilisation and the dark night of barbarism.

In the spring of 161 Antoninus, now seventy-five years old, died as he had lived—calmly and with dignity, entrusting the Empire to his adopted son Marcus Aurelius in the presence of his senior officers. As a symbol of this inheritance, he gave Marcus the golden statue of the goddess Fortune, which had always stood in the emperor's bedroom. His last task was to give the night's watchword to the officer of the guard. In what seemed a final expression of faith, he gave the word 'Equanimity', turned over as if to sleep and so died. Like Julius Caesar himself, he had so impressed his own qualities upon the office of emperor that many of his successors took his name, Antoninus; and his title of Pius was used as long as emperors ruled in Rome.

Marcus Aurelius Antoninus Caesar was forty when he succeeded, and proved himself not unworthy of his great inheritance or of the name Antoninus. He had married the latter's daughter Faustina and had been carefully trained for the great office he was to fill. Born in Rome, he was a grave and studious child, and continued to find time for scholarship during his busy manhood. He studied philosophy under Junius Rusticus, whom he twice honoured with the Consulship. It seemed that Plato's golden age had come, when the world would be governed by men trained in philosophy. Marcus often referred to this fact, for he himself was a follower of the Stoic doctrine, one of the noblest schemes of thought produced by the ancient world. He was author of a book, *The Meditations*, which he wrote while on campaign in the East, and which still speaks to us with the quiet voice of reason and moderation. Marcus Aurelius appointed his brother, Lucius Aurelius Verus Commodus Caesar, as his colleague, so that Rome for the first time had two men with the hitherto unique title of Augustus. This, as we shall see, was to furnish a precedent for future ages.

His reign opened at a time when the long peace of Antoninus was drawing to an end. There was a growing threat of barbarian invasions along many of the frontiers and war appeared to be imminent in Britain. We do not know the precise nature of the troubles, but their seriousness is suggested by the fact that Marcus immediately appointed a new Governor, who bore the historic name of Agricola. He was active in northern Britain and more than one inscription on Hadrian's Wall bears his name. Some seven or eight years later (probably in 169) there was a further campaign in the island. It was at this time that Marcus sent some 5,000 cavalrymen to reinforce the garrison in Britain. These came from Southern Russia, settled in the province, and added yet another thread to the tapestry of Britain's population.

Despite the difficulties which Rome now faced (there were border troubles from the Adriatic to the Atlantic, an invasion of Spain by the Moors, and a widespread epidemic), his reign was long remembered as a time of happiness and justice. Gibbon wrote that, during the reigns of Antoninus Pius and Marcus Aurelius, the aims of government were for the first time the happiness of the people.

In 178 he and his son Commodus left Rome for Pannonia (the modern Austria), and for the next two or three years he was continually on campaign. In 180 he fell sick, the war unfinished. Commodus had already shown himself an unworthy heir and knowledge of this clouded his last days. He feared that on his death his son would terminate the war, and, ill as he was, he begged him to continue the campaign. Despite these misgivings, he sought to hasten death by refusing both food and drink, and true to his Stoic faith, rebuked his friends for weeping, commanding them rather to think of the plague in which so many thousands had perished, and how death was the common lot of mortal man. He died peacefully in his sleep, universally mourned as one whom power had not corrupted and who had proved, by his constant virtues, the truth of what he himself had written: that a man may lead a good life, even in a palace. It was later said that, towards the end, he expressed the hope that Commodus would die, since he could foresee the disasters that Commodus would bring to the state after his own death. He did not want to be succeeded by one who might become another Nero, Caligula or Domitian. His wish was denied him and his prophecy woefully fulfilled.

Marcus Aurelius had striven to give Commodus the best of education and the finest of tutors, but the boy had given early evidence of cruelty. One day, when he was only twelve, his bath was too cold and he ordered the servant to be burned alive in the bath furnace. Only the resourcefulness of a fellow servant who threw a sheepskin into the fire, which gave off a black and acrid smoke, saved the wretched slave from a hideous death. Commodus grew up to be lustful and totally depraved. When he came to power, he peopled the palace with prostitutes of both sexes, drawn both from the common people and from the aristocracy. As governors of the provinces he chose his own vicious friends and the boon companions of his orgies.

His biographer tells us something of his British wars and how 'the barbarians in the island crossed the Wall which divides them from the Roman camps and caused a great deal of damage'. They killed a Roman commander and the men under his command. Alpius Marcellus, who had been Governor of Britain during the earlier years of Commodus's reign, was sent back to Britain to deal with the emergency. He was a stern and ruthless soldier and utterly routed the barbarians who had broken into the province. It is probable that the wall referred to was the Antonine Wall and that the invasion of the barbarians was limited to the lowlands of Scotland.

Commodus was acclaimed as Imperator, struck a coin to commemorate his victory in Britain, and bestowed upon himself the new title of Britannicus. The Romans had always bestowed upon their victorious generals names embodying those of the nations they had vanquished. Thus Commodus Britannicus, though unworthy, was in his own eyes now to be classed with Scipio Africanus of the Punic Wars and the heroic Germanicus. One memorial of his reign still remains in Britain. From Carlisle there comes an inscription, dedicating an altar or temple 'To the Divine Companions of the God Hercules'; Commodus was not content to claim a prowess equal to that of great men of the past, but identified himself with Hercules, son of Jove.

During the reign of Commodus we begin to see how the remote island of Britain, permanently manned by a powerful garrison of three legions, could be a threat to Roman security. An ambitious commander could, whenever times were troubled, intervene forcefully in the politics of the Empire. There had been a hint of this during AD 69, as we have seen, when the garrison in Britain threw its weight behind Vitellius. Now there was to be clearer evidence of Britain's growing influence. Among Commodus's most unworthy officers was a man named Perennis, who is said to have encouraged Commodus to devote his life to limitless debauchery so that he himself might take the reins of government into his own hands. The evidence is conflicting: Lampridius says roundly that he plundered numerous citizens, subverting all the laws and enriching himself thereby; Dio, on the other hand, says that he acted with honesty and moderation. Whatever the truth of the matter, his regime was highly unpopular. The army in Britain, secure behind its moat of the Channel, first planned to appoint its own emperor, but then changed its mind, though still planning to end the tyranny in Rome. Dio reports that it sent a delegation of 1,500 soldiers to Rome to demand the dismissal of Perennis. These men, by demonstrating their determination and by reminding Rome of the strength of Britain's garrison, helped to procure the downfall of the hated minister.

There seems little doubt that Commodus was insane, his madness taking the form of delusions of grandeur. Since he was already absolute Emperor there was little scope for illusions of further greatness; but Commodus solved this psychological problem by identifying himself (as we have seen) with the god Hercules. On some of his coins he wears the skin of the Nemean lion and carries the club of Hercules. He turned the month of October into the month of Hercules and changed the names of other months. He also planned to change the name of Rome to The Commodian Colony.

His favourite concubine was a Christian named Marcia. In the end, sickened by his vices, she and the Prefect of the Praetorian Guard poisoned him, but the potion they used was ineffective and the poor wretch did not die. So, before he could recover from his sickness they had him strangled. His squalid death took place in 192, after twelve years of power and debauchery, by which time Rome's majestic advance under the Antonines had been halted, and the Empire was in disarray—much as it had been after the death of Nero.

Emperors now bore three titles: Caesar, bestowed upon them either by adoption or by declaration after conquest, which provided a fictional thread of dynastic continuity; Augustus, the designation given to Octavian and to each succeeding emperor; and Imperator or commander-in-chief of the armies, from which our word emperor derives. This last title was bestowed upon an emperor by the acclamation of his troops after a notable victory, and gave great power to the soldiers. The significance of this was first shown after the murder of Caligula, when they alone had secured the accession of Claudius. Most influential of all army units was the Praetorian Guard, originally the bodyguard of the Praetors, but under Augustus becoming the Emperor's household troops. The *praefectus* (or Colonel) of the guard acquired massive influence as protector and adviser of the reigning Augustus. So powerful was the office that centuries later, when the

G

Roman Empire had dissolved and only a shadow empire persisted in Byzantium, the title of Praetorian Prefect was borne
by the chief ministers of the Byzantine Emperors.

When Commodus died, the Senate bestowed the diadem and
the title of Augustus upon Pertinax, an elderly soldier who
had achieved senatorial rank as a result of a successful military
career, and who was now Prefect of the City. Earlier he had
served in Britain, where Antoninus had appointed him to a
senior command as a reward for his services during the
Parthian Wars. About 184 Commodus had sent Pertinax back
to Britain as Governor. His military reputation must then have
stood high, for the fierce campaign of Marcellus had but
recently been fought and the island was in need of a firm hand
and a forceful commander. Pertinax was successful and thus
another future emperor had enhanced his reputation by service
in the province of Britain.

Like Vespasian, whose background was so similar and who
had inherited problems similar to his own, Pertinax began a
programme of strict economy and reform. The Praetorian
Guard found his discipline too harsh and his austerity unacceptable and, after he had reigned only twelve weeks, they
murdered him. Their trust betrayed, their arms tarnished
with the blood of the man it was their duty to protect, the
character of the Praetorian Guard was now irrevocably
changed. Henceforth they were not so much the protectors as
the makers of emperors.

There followed one of the most disgraceful episodes in the
long history of the Praetorians. They triumphantly brought
the head of the murdered Pertinax into their barracks impaled
upon a spear. Pertinax's father-in-law, Sulpicianus, saw himself as the natural successor of his dead son-in-law, but the
Praetorians, remembering the bounty they had always received on the accession of a new Augustus (a pattern set by
Claudius), demurred. They publicly announced that they would
bestow the Empire upon the man who offered them the
highest price. There followed a squalid public auction for the
post of ruler of the world. The bids lay between Sulpicianus
and Didius Julianus, a wealthy senator. The two stood under

the barrack ramparts making their bids and Julianus finally won the day with an offer of 25,000 sesterces for every guardsman. Returning from the barracks, Julianus passed the headless and bleeding body of Pertinax, which he callously disregarded, and spent a night of feasting to celebrate his empty success. But the people despised him and rejected his rule. An appeal was sent to Pescennius Niger, who was then Governor of Syria and a former Consul. He was acclaimed Imperator and Augustus by his troops but stayed on in Syria, the first man to bear the title of Emperor in lands far from the City of Rome. At the same time two other provincial Governors, seeing the state in disarray and realising that their own troops could both acclaim and defend them, declared themselves Emperor and took the name of Caesar.

One of these was Clodius Albinus, who had been born in Africa. He had joined the army as a young man and had received successive promotions until, during the reign of Commodus, he had been appointed Governor of Britain. For the first but not the last time Britain had put forward her own Emperor and was now playing a full part in the politics of the Empire.

Albinus is said to have been given that name because as a baby he was whiter than his linen swaddling clothes. He spent his childhood in his native Africa, joining the army while still in his teens. His abilities were noticed by the two Antonines and, as military tribune, he was given command of a troop of cavalry from Dalmatia (the modern Yugoslavia). He later commanded the First and Fourth Legions in Moesia (between modern Yugoslavia and the Black Sea); and during the reign of Commodus he was transferred to Gaul, where he defeated an attempted invasion of the province by the Germans from across the Rhine. It was as a reward for this success that Commodus is said to have contemplated making him his heir.

About 190 he was appointed Governor of Britain, where he had three legions at his command—the Second at Caerleon-on-Usk in Monmouthshire, the Twentieth Victorious at Chester and the Sixth at York. With its auxiliaries, this formidable army had already shown its power in the affair of Perennis. A governor of Britain, provided he was willing to ignore his loyalty to the central government, could with little difficulty obtain the title, if not the metropolitan office, of Emperor.

While Albinus watched events in Rome and saw with increasing clarity the opportunities for his own ambition, another provincial governor made a separate bid for power. This was Septimius Severus, Governor of Pannonia. In reply to appeals from Rome he marched his troops across the Alps and down to Ravenna, where he seized a fleet. Meanwhile, Julianus, whose sordid purchase of the Empire had so enraged the people, was unable to organise any effective resistance. Severus's armies entered the capital and Julianus was killed in the palace by a soldier. He died pathetically beseeching 'the protection of Caesar', that is to say of Severus, who was now formally declared Emperor by the Senate.

Severus had first to consolidate his own position before dealing with his rival Albinus by open opposition. Using guile as a weapon, he ostensibly recognised Albinus's claim and wrote to him in Britain, greeting him with the name of Caesar and inviting him to rule the Empire as a brother. The messengers who brought the letter had in fact been instructed by Severus to seek a private audience with Albinus and to assassinate him, but the plot was discovered and the messengers put to the torture.

To make good his claim Albinus knew that he must cross to the mainland of Europe and fight. Accordingly he led the garrisons of Britain across the Channel, which shows that the British Fleet was still in being. Severus took up the challenge and a bitter battle for the Empire was fought outside Lyons. For the first time the armies of Britain had drawn their swords in a struggle for world power. Although defeated, they did not learn circumspection, and during the following century the armies of Britain were to set out on many similar adventures.

During the absence of the garrison the northern defences of

Britain were overrun by the barbarians. Excavation has shown that much of Hadrian's Wall was destroyed about this time, the timbers burned and the massive stonework overturned.

The barbarian tide seems to have swept south to York, where there are signs of the destruction of the walls, and south-west to Chester.

At Lyons Albinus saw his ambitions fade in the fearful clamour of battle and defeat. The fighting was savage and it was said that the Rhône ran red with blood. When all was lost he stabbed himself and was dragged, dying, before the triumphant Severus. His body, once so proudly dressed in the purple of imperial authority lay disregarded in front of Severus's headquarters for many days until the ambitious flesh had rotted away, and it was finally flung contemptuously into the turbulent waters of the Rhône. So ended Britain's first dream of setting up an emperor. Severus was now master of the world both by the acclaim of his troops and by his victory over his rival. Gibbon dates the decline of Rome from Severus's triumph, for it was he who first brought to the Empire the eastern concepts of government whereby the Emperor was seen as the owner and not the protector of his people, and the muscular reality of power was to be clothed in the luxurious garment of courtly ritual.

Severus was born in the city of Leptis in North Africa, where the ruined town (with its theatre, shops and jetty) stands to this day, white in the hot sunshine, preserved by the dry air of the surrounding desert. As a young man he left Africa to seek a career in Rome, and was promoted to senatorial rank by Marcus Aurelius. He was sponsored by a kinsman named Septimius Severus, whose name he took. His biographer, whose evidence, however, is not reliable, says that he lived riotously and faced at least one charge of adultery. What is certain is that he duly became Quaestor in Rome, later serving as Quaestor in Sardinia and then on the staff of the proconsul of Africa. Back in Rome he was promoted Tribune of the People by Marcus Aurelius, and it was at this time that he married his first wife, Marciana. Then, when he was thirty-two, he received the rank of Praetor and was thereafter appointed Propraetor of Spain. His real military career began with his promotion to the command of the Fourth Legion, nicknamed the Scythian, which was then stationed near Marseilles. After a tour of Greece he was appointed as Legate to Lyons.

Marciana died and in 173 he married a remarkable woman named Julia Domna, a Syrian by birth and daughter of Bassianus, high priest of the sun god, Elagabalus. She bore him two sons, Marcus Aurelius Antoninus and Septimius Geta. She was a gifted woman of dominating personality, who was to become his colleague, sharing the responsibilities of government. After his appointment in Gaul he served as proconsul in Pannonia and later in Sicily. By now Commodus was emperor, and a charge was brought against Severus (possibly at the instigation of Commodus) of consulting soothsayers and astrologers about the possibility of inheriting the Empire. His judges acquitted him and his accuser (perhaps seen by the judges as a creature of the hated Commodus) suffered the cruel death of crucifixion.

Severus returned to Rome, became Consul, and was then appointed commander of the armies in Pannonia. It was there that news came of the death of Commodus, the murder of Pertinax, and the shameful election of Julianus. Severus, acclaimed emperor by his own legions, gave each man 1,000 sesterces, and marched on Rome. The armies of Illyria and Gaul followed his standards. Declared a public enemy by the desperate Julianus, he resumed his advance and, on the death of Julianus, became Emperor in 193 under the name of Caesar Lucius Septimius Severus Pertinax.

He entered Rome not as liberator but as conqueror. The senators who came to offer him the empire were searched for hidden weapons, and he greeted them fully armed and surrounded by his armed supporters. Still in armour, he marched to the Capitol and thence to the palace, surrounded by the standards of his legions. His admiration for Pertinax was demonstrated by his adoption of the dead Emperor's name: his abhorrence of the murder by his dissolution of the Praetorian guard.

After thus ordering matters in Rome he advanced against Pescennius Niger, Governor of Syria, who had assumed the title of Caesar Augustus. Many in Rome supported Niger, whose reputation as a strict and able general made him a dangerous rival. Severus fought two battles against him in Asia Minor and was finally victorious. The head of Niger was paraded on a spear, his wife and children slaughtered, and his family entirely wiped out. As we have seen, Severus then turned to the West and defeated Albinus at Lyons.

Two years after his accession, Severus led an army to the eastern frontiers, crossed the Euphrates and assumed the title of *Parthicus*—conqueror of the Parthians. He captured Byzantium, the ancient city on the narrow sea dividing Europe from Asia, which was to become the future Constantinople. He spent the next three or four years in the East, striving to settle frontier problems that earlier emperors had failed to resolve. With his two sons he captured Babylon and tried twice to capture Atra in Arabia, where Trajan had taken his mortal sickness. Meanwhile he was content for others to rule in Rome.

Julius Caesar, by conquering Gaul, had secured for Rome the wide Atlantic as her western frontier. To the east the Rhine and Danube provided natural barriers against the barbarians beyond, and Augustus had defined these rivers as the limits of the Empire. South of the African provinces there lay mile after mile of forest, peopled by nations too primitive to defy the Eagles of Rome, and a wide sweep of desert. Only upon the frontiers of the middle East was there perpetual peril. The warlike Parthians threatened Rome's grip upon her eastern provinces, and, after their incorporation in the Persian empire in the first quarter of the second century, the danger to Rome remained.

In the north, Britain was Rome's outpost. With the lands south of Hadrian's Wall fully Romanised, Rome's frontier now lay on the Wall. It says much for the growing importance of Britain that in 207 Severus left the troubled eastern frontier, marched westwards, crossed the narrow seas, and with his two sons landed in the island of Britain. He was the first

reigning Augustus to do so since Hadrian, over eighty years
earlier.

Rutupiae (Richborough), where Claudius had landed, was
now a busy port and it was probably here that he stepped
ashore. To cross the Thames he would have journeyed to
London, now a walled city with fine public buildings, temples
to many gods, busy wharves and jetties, and offices where
government clerks laboured on the endless work of administer-
ing the province. Northwards lay the road to York, military
headquarters of the frontier area. Severus and his sons traversed
this road, through green woodlands, rich pastures and rolling
moorlands. Beyond the Wall, rebuilt by Severus's Governors,
the tribes were still unconquered, and Severus now determined
on a punitive expedition to pacify the northern frontier of the
Empire. Two nations in particular had to be taught a final
lesson: the Caledonii of the Highlands and the Meatae of the
Lowlands of what is now Scotland. Severus's Governors
repaired the Wall so thoroughly that, in folk memory, he was
long remembered as the builder of it, his reputation over-
topping Hadrian's.

Like Agricola before him Severus led an army into
Caledonia and, like Agricola, failed to make any permanent
lodgement there. His campaign was pursued vigorously
enough. He led his troops resolutely across the harsh countryside. Where there were marshy valleys they built causeways;
where there were wide rivers they constructed bridges. And
always there was the enemy, lurking in the forests, hiding in
the heather, ambushing stragglers in the deep glens. The
discipline of the legions never faltered, even though they had
been trained to fight in pitched battles, face to face and
sword to sword. But here, in the fine rain of the Highlands,
against enemies for the most part unseen, such training was of
little direct help. But discipline prevailed: they never gave
up, holding together and marching stubbornly forward. Many
died and all were weary, and Severus himself, now in his
sixties, was a sick and indeed a dying man.

In the winter of 210-11 he ordered the withdrawal of his
tired army. Severus was taken back to York, where in February

211 he died, after a reign of eighteen years. He was the first Emperor to die in Britain, but his bones do not lie in the island. His body was cremated and the ashes carried reverently to Rome and there placed, with great solemnity, in the tomb of his great predecessor Marcus Aurelius. He had not conquered Caledonia, but the frontier remained peaceful for almost 100 years after his death.

IV · SEVERVS TO THE ACCESSION OF DIOCLETIAN

Alien Emperors, Usurpation and Decay -
Third Century AD

The manner of Severus's accession demonstrated that power now rarely passed smoothly to a designated heir, and the office of Augustus in the third century became more and more a prize to be fought for by ambitious men. During the first and second centuries there were twelve and eight emperors respectively, but during the third there were to be more than sixty. The imperial system suffered increasing instability as ambitious military commanders struggled to achieve that dazzling position.

Severus left two sons, Marcus Antoninus and Septimius Geta. Marcus, the elder, had been born at Lyons during one of his father's campaigns and was twenty-three when Severus died. Geta, who had been born in Rome, was a year younger. Each received the title of Augustus from their dying father, whose wish it was that both should govern as equal colleagues. Originally the elder had been named Bassianus after his grandfather, the Syrian priest of Elagabalus the Sun God, but

Severus changed it to Marcus Aurelius Antoninus to match his son's imperial destiny. However, it was not by that name that he was known either to his people or to history. In Gaul, where he had spent much time, the men wore long ankle-length cloaks with hoods; he considered these extremely practical garments, wore one himself and introduced them as part of the army's equipment. The Gaulish name for such a cloak was Caracalla and this became his nickname.

As a boy, Caracalla had shown great promise: he was studious at school, generous to his friends and so full of compassion (and this was surprising to the Romans, who rejoiced in the sight of blood) that he would avert his eyes when he saw condemned criminals thrown to the wild beasts in the arena. When he was only seven, one of his friends had been thrashed for adopting the Jewish religion, and Caracalla was so upset by the harshness of the punishment that for a long time he would speak neither to his father nor to his friend's father. But as he grew up, youthful virtue fell away and he revealed himself as a man of cruel and ruthless ambition. He spared no one, not even his own brother, in his merciless quest for absolute power.

After the cremation of Severus at York, Caracalla and Geta left Britain with the dead Emperor's ashes. Although both were young, each had gained distinction in the island province. During the last campaign, Caracalla rather than Severus had been in active command of the troops, while Geta, according to some authorities, acted as governor in the south. As they travelled the roads of Gaul, each of the imperial brothers was received in the provincial cities with equal honour, since both held the supreme office of Augustus. But even on this sad journey (upon which they were marching not merely with the majesty of their rank but with the mournful solemnity befitting those bearing the ashes of the dead Augustus), rivalry between the brothers began to be apparent.

For cruelty and ambition there was little to choose between them. Geta, the handsomer and more tragic figure, had no more compassion than his better known brother. When he was a mere youth, hearing of his father's decision to execute many political opponents (particularly the followers of the defeated Clodius Albinus), he pressed for the death of their parents and all their kinsmen, so that none might survive to resent the killings. Caracalla had been content to recommend to his father the slaughter only of the children of the condemned men! Geta drank deeply, pursued many amorous adventures, and indulged in affectation even in his luxury. He would arrange dinner parties where all the dishes alliterated; so that pullets, partridge, peacock and pork would all be served at table. He was learned, but more given to quibbles than to scholarship. He had a pleasant speaking voice marred by a slight stammer.

Caracalla believed, or purported to believe, that Geta was plotting against him. Once the brothers reached Rome and had laid the ashes of Severus reverently in Hadrian's tomb, Caracalla ordered his brother's assassination, and the young man was murdered in the arms of his mother, twelve brief months after the death of Severus in Britain. Caracalla now exercised undivided rule, but, conscious of his guilt and of the odium that the appalling sin of fratricide would bring upon him, he hastened to justify his bloody act. From the palace, where the corpse of Geta lay, he hastened straight to the barracks of the Praetorian Guard, knowing that they now held the gift of Empire in their hands and that without their support no Emperor could survive. He told them that Geta had conspired against him, had planned to poison him, and had been treating his mother insolently. He paid tribute to Geta's murderers and publicly rewarded them. Not all the troops believed him. The Second Legion (the Parthican) recalled its oath to both the sons of Severus and refused to admit Caracalla to its camp. He was able to pacify them only after redoubling his recriminations against his dead brother, and by offering them a large increase in pay.

The Senate also had to be won over. Caracalla knew that his act of violence might bring violent retribution, even in the chamber of the Senate, so when he attended the house on the day following the murder, he wore a breastplate beneath his toga and was accompanied by armed troops. These were drawn up between the benches and only when he had thus overawed the senators did he address them. Again he accused his brother of treachery and ingratitude, but it was said that he spoke hesitatingly and without conviction. The Senate reluctantly accepted his arguments, reinforced as these were by the menace of the stern soldiers.

Then followed a series of judicial murders as Caracalla destroyed all his brother's friends, seeking in a frenzy of violence to wash away his own blood-guilt in the abundant blood of his victims. Senators were executed or forced to commit suicide; assassins made away with his cousin Afer, who was brutally murdered after breaking his legs in a desperate attempt to escape from a high window; and learned men, nobles who had held high office, and men of consular rank were indiscriminately slaughtered by his agents.

In the spring of 213, he set out for Gaul and there continued his policy of butchery, executing the proconsul in Narbonne and behaving ruthlessly towards the provincials. But on his expedition he also waged successful war: he defeated the Alemanni, fought his way into the unsubdued German lands and won a great victory on the River Main. He assumed the title of *Germanicus Maximus* and issued coins commemorating his victory. He also struck coins of silver and bronze in honour of his campaigns in Britain; one shows a winged Victory and another depicts Victory facing the now familiar figure of Britannia.

After returning to Rome, he marched eastwards through Dacia into Thrace, crossed to Asia, nearly perishing in a shipwreck, and visited Egypt. In Alexandria he began to show increasing signs of madness, for he enrolled men into his army and then had them slaughtered, and ordered his troops to butcher the peaceful householders upon whom they were billeted. Later he marched against the Babylonians and fought Rome's perpetual foes the Parthians, adding the title of *Parthicus* to his many dignities. With him on his campaigns was an ambitious man named Opellius Macrinus, who had once been his private steward and who now held the rank of Colonel of the Praetorian Guard. Macrinus was responsible for the civil administration, while Adventus, who held the same rank, was military commander. Jealousy between these two, rumours that an African sorcerer had predicted Macrinus would one day be Emperor, together with growing resentment in the court against Caracalla's cruelty, were enough in those troubled and unstable days to engender a plot against him.

Caracalla spent the winter of 217-18 in Mesopotamia. On his birthday in April 217 he ordered the citizens of Carrhae to attend a ceremony in honour of the Semitic moon god. As the grandson of Bassianus, the Syrian priest of the Sun God, he had more than a passing interest in attending these rites, and rode out with his bodyguard in holiday mood, not knowing that he was riding to his death. Among the guard was a soldier named Martialis, who had been refused promotion by the Emperor and, therefore, bore him a grudge. Martialis had made common cause with Macrinus, with two brothers who were Tribunes of the Guard, and with the commander of the Second (Parthican) Legion, that which had so reluctantly accepted Caracalla and in which opposition to him still smouldered. After a while, Caracalla called a halt and dismounted, and as he did so, Martialis left the ranks, drew his dagger and plunged it into Caracalla's side. The Emperor fell dying in the spring sunshine, his blood seeping into the yellow sand. There was a great shout from the soldiers: 'Martialis has done it!' Then a Scythian cavalryman, faithful to his dead Emperor, advanced upon Martialis and cut him down.

Rome and the Senate lay many days' journey from the dusty road where the corpse of Caracalla lay, and long before news could reach the senators (who, in theory at least, had the power to appoint a successor) the armies and the court alike had, for want of a better, hailed Macrinus as Augustus, and the dangerous prophecy of the African sorcerer was fulfilled.

Macrinus himself had been born in north Africa fifty-three years earlier, in humble circumstances. Indeed, there were malicious rumours that he was a freed slave and that, during the reign of Commodus, he had lived as a male prostitute. There is no reason to believe these stories, but certainly his birth was less than noble, and we first meet him as an obscure lawyer. His coins show an undistinguished face with a long pointed nose, and a receding chin which a full beard fails to disguise. When news of his accession reached Rome the Senate grudgingly confirmed him as Augustus, declaring that they would prefer anyone to Caracalla the fratricide, the incestuous, the impure, the butcher of Senate and people. The army in the east, which had acclaimed him, did so with a like coolness and he never enjoyed their full affection or permanent loyalty. He was an unyielding disciplinarian, executing soldiers by crucifixion, a punishment usually reserved for slaves and criminals. To consolidate his position he took the revered name of Antoninus, and sought to gain the loyalty of Adventus (his former rival) by entrusting him with the task of bearing back to Rome the remains of Caracalla, there to be buried with all pomp. In his own formal despatch to the Senate he reported Caracalla's death and swore that he knew nothing of the killing.

He had a nine year old son, Diadumenian, upon whom he bestowed the name of Caesar, advancing him to the rank of Augustus in the following year. Coins were issued bearing the boy's portrait and the title of *Princeps Juventutis*, leader of the youth. Realising that he could not be sure of his army's loyalty, and that disaffection grows more rapidly among idle troops than among those on active service, he led them forth-with against the Parthians. They were given no time either to judge him or to spread rumours about the violent manner of his accession, for Caracalla, despite his evil ways, had been loved by the legionaries.

Meanwhile Julia Maesa, sister of Julia Domna and sister-in-law of the dead Septimius Severus, saw an opportunity of restoring the Empire to the descendants of her father Bass-ianus, the Syrian priest. She realised that Macrinus had been but grudgingly accepted by the Senate; that he was unknown to the citizens of Rome; that the army of Syria, upon whose support his power was based, held him in little esteem; and that the troops still remembered Caracalla with affection. In all this she glimpsed imperial possibilities for her twelve year old grandson, the son of her daughter Julia Soaemias. The boy had inherited from his great-grandfather Bassianus the office of High Priest of the Syrian Sun God Elagabalus, and it is by the god's name that he is himself known. His mother had been married to Sextus Varius Marcellus and the boy's true name was Varius. But his ambitious grandmother put about the story that he was really Caracalla's son, not hesitating to impugn her daughter's chastity if by so doing she could further the boy's advancement. (The accusation of adultery, though false in this instance, was not unmerited, for Dio tells us that Julia Soaemias had had a love affair with her son's tutor.) The rumour of the boy's imperial birth was eagerly believed by the army, which yearned for a return to the stability of a hereditary Augustus.

The ambition of Julia Maesa was sharpened by resentment, for she had now been expelled from the Palace. The Third (Gaulish) Legion was stationed near Emesa in Syria, birthplace of her sister and cradle of her family, and there she went to spread the tale of her grandson's imperial birth. She took the boy into the camp, where the soldiers hailed him as Antoninus, presenting him with their standards and so declaring him Emperor.

The news reached Macrinus while he was with his armies near Antioch, and at first he did not take the defection of one legion seriously, particularly as it was a mere woman who had moved the revolt. He was content to send Julianus, Prefect of the Praetorian Guard, with an expeditionary force to subdue the Third Legion. But Julianus's troops, when the boy was shown to them as Caracalla's son, acclaimed him with great enthusiasm. They turned on Julianus and slew him, declaring their support for Varius Antoninus—the young Elagabalus. It was now June 218 and the Third Legion, with its unexpected reinforcements, moved to the offensive. Macrinus led his troops out of Antioch to meet them and the two armies met some 25 miles from that city, under the burning summer sun.

Perhaps Macrinus's own troops fought half-heartedly, moved by discipline rather than loyalty. Long before the battle was ended, Macrinus knew that victory was deserting his standards and, with his son Diadumenian, he fled the field. He sent the boy, with a small body of troops, to the king of Parthia for protection, but he himself was captured at Chalcedon on the Bosphorus by a troop of soldiers and put to death. Meanwhile Diadumenian was also taken and killed. So ended the brief and unsuccessful reign of Macrinus the African and so began the reign of Elagabalus the Syrian.

Despatches were sent to Rome in his name and received with enthusiasm by the Senate. He bore the revered name of Antoninus and was held to be the son of Caracalla who—for all his cruelty—had been Emperor by descent and not by conquest. His reign opened with brilliant hope. The city, sickened by the bloodshed and battles of the past, looked forward eagerly to a new golden age under this handsome young kinsman of the great Septimius Severus. But city and army alike were to be woefully disappointed. If the decline of the Empire began with the death of Aurelius, it became hideously apparent with the accession of Elagabalus. Rome's first shock was his setting up of a temple to the Syrian god Elagabalus on the Palatine hill, close to the houses of the Caesars, where he enshrined an ancient stone, the embodiment of the deity, which he had brought from Emesa. Into the temple of this alien god he blasphemously sought to bring the image of the Great Mother, the sacred fire of Vesta and all those objects the Romans had for generations considered most holy. He also ordered the rites of the Jews and Christians to be performed in the same temple so that the priests of the Sun God might be masters of every religion of the Empire.

But a greater scandal than his blasphemy against Rome's hallowed beliefs was his limitless and obscene lust. Still only a boy, he left the government in the hands of his mother and grandmother, while he himself indulged every outrageous fantasy a depraved imagination could conceive. He spent the winter of 218-19 in Nicomedia and there, to his soldier's horror, he revealed himself as a homosexual of insatiable appetite. Men's minds began to see a possible alternative in Alexander, son of Julia Maesa's younger daughter Julia Mammaea, and thus cousin to the vicious Elagabulus. How

H

could the people tolerate an Augustus whose thoughts were concerned only with finding sensuous pleasures for every part of his body—behaving in ways which even a beast would shun?

Back in Rome he continued upon his monstrous course. The city was scoured by his agents for the most muscular and virile men, who were brought to the palace so that he might be enjoyed by them. The house of the Caesars, from which the great and virtuous had once ruled the world, was now polluted by this boy. His face painted like a whore's, he would strut in the part of Venus in a play, dropping his women's clothes to stand naked before the audience, in a ghastly caricature of the classical statues of the goddess, with buttocks thrust grotesquely backwards, one hand covering his breast and the other placed in obscene mock modesty. He sold honours and powers, which other Caesars had given as rewards for merit, for cash or allowed his favourites to sell them. To his other deviations he added the monstrous practice of fellatio with Hierocles, a former slave.

In 219, when he was still only fourteen, Elagabalus married Julia Cornelia Paula, who received the title of Augusta. Coins were issued with her portrait, many bearing the slogan *Concordia*, but the concord of the marriage was short-lived. A year later he divorced her, and, to Rome's horror, married Julia Aquilia, one of the Vestal Virgins. This was both profanation and incest. Some said that he had raped Aquilia. Since he was not only a homosexual, but a passive one, this seems unlikely. More probably he now saw himself not so much the Emperor as the personification of the Sun God, whom all mankind must worship. By marrying a Vestal Virgin he was, as it were, subordinating Rome's state religion to his own cult.

About this time he also became a devotee of the goddess Cybele and, as was the practice of her followers, castrated himself. He was now not merely a transvestite but a pathetic half-man, at once the exploiter and victim of his own lust, and a degraded plaything of other men. One of his favourites was an athlete from Smyrna named Aurelius Zoticus, with whom he went through a wedding ceremony. They had intercourse and Elagabalus always looked upon Zoticus as his husband. He surrounded himself with people of similar tastes: a dancer became Prefect of the Guard, a racing-chariot driver was Prefect of the Watch, and a barber was placed in charge of Rome's corn supply.

In 221, still only sixteen, he divorced Aquilia and married Anna Faustina, but this marriage lasted only a few months and he went back to Aquilia. In the same year he adopted his cousin Alexander as his son; since Alexander was a mere three years younger than himself, the adoption was quite simply the nomination of an heir. The initiative could hardly have been the Emperor's, for a lad of sixteen would not normally be concerned with selecting a successor. His mother, or perhaps his grandmother, must have realised that Elagabalus had effectively destroyed himself as Emperor, and that the sole hope of retaining power for the dynasty lay in young Alexander. The gold coin bearing the new Caesar's portrait carried the figure of Hope. Elagabalus angrily resented the adoption of his cousin, ordering Alexander's new statues to be insulted, and their inscriptions to be defaced with mud. The troops, with whom Alexander was immensely popular, heard (or invented) a rumour that he was to be murdered, and took him with his mother and grandmother to the safety of their own camp. They planned to kill Elagabalus but then offered to strike a bargain with him instead: his life would be spared provided he dismissed the most notorious of his evil companions, Hierocles, and two others. Some kind of compromise was reached and in the winter Elagabalus and Alexander were both appointed Consuls. But at the last minute Elagabalus refused to appear with his cousin. Persisting in his plan to murder Alexander, but fearing that the Senate would nominate another heir, he dismissed that venerable body.

The troops, and in particular the Praetorian Guard, decided the time had come to put an end to their perverted Emperor, and broke into the palace, slaughtering with dreadful tortures many of Elagabalus's boon companions. Poor Elagabulas (and monster though he was, pity for this frightened and mutilated boy cannot be withheld) had for nearly three years been the prisoner of his own vice and of the temptations offered by unlimited wealth and privilege. With ruthless soldiers storming through his house, and with the blood of his lovers staining the white marble and bright mosaics of the imperial rooms, he hid himself fearfully in one of the palace latrines. There the soldiers found him and there they butchered him, then dragged his bloody corpse through the city as a public show. Eventually it was thrust into a sewer, but the sewer would not receive it. Thereupon the soldiers, after dragging it once more round the Circus, weighted it and threw it into the River Tiber, so that it might have neither the decency of burial nor the rites of religion.

It must have been evident to all that the real rulers of the Empire were Elagabalus's mother and grandmother, the ambitious descendants of the high priest Bassianus, and outward signs of their power were not wanting. His mother, against all precedent, had been admitted to the Senate and to a place on the consular benches. A woman's senate had been set up, to the great scandal of conservative Rome. Yet somehow the women of the family escaped the odium of the people, for, after the death of Elagabalus they were able to continue their rule through the boy Alexander.

The Senate invited the new Emperor to attend a special session, where they acclaimed him Augustus, and gave him the title of Father of the Country, a strange designation for a boy of fourteen, and one which former emperors had usually received after several years of power. Alexander was also appointed *Pontifex Maximus* and given both the consular and tribunician powers. The Senate was demonstrating not only its relief at the death of Elagabalus, but the fact that it and not the army was the sovereign body. Too many emperors had recently been appointed at the caprice of the Legions. By giving so speedily all the imperial insignia to Alexander the Senate emphasised its own authority and left nothing for the army to bestow, save its loyalty and protection.

Alexander declined one honour—the name Antoninus. It had been so besmirched by his predeccessor that it was never used by any emperor again.

Alexander had been born at Arca Caesarea, close to the modern Tripoli, and carefully educated; but, coming from the eastern lands of the Empire, he was more at home with Greek than Latin. He was tall, handsome and had the bearing—even in his youth—of a soldier. His mother, Julia Mammaea, at first took all decisions in his name, but she did not fall into the same trap as her sister, who had retained power through her son's preoccupation with depravity. Julia Mammaea ensured that the government was conducted with decorum and moderation, and was also careful to instil like doctrines in the mind of Alexander. All traces of Elagabalus were swept away. The statues and relics of the ancient gods were reverently replaced in the temples from which Elagabalus had so blasphemously removed them.

When Julia Maesa died, she was given all the honours normally reserved for a reigning emperor. This was fitting, for it was by her resolution that the dynasty of Bassianus had been established. Julia Mammaea continued to rule Alexander. She placed the palace under strict surveillance, ensuring that no persons of evil reputation should join his household. She encouraged him to carry out the duties of his office, and to spend much of his time on judicial matters. She also chose his bride, Orbiana (the daughter of a Senator), whom he married some three years after coming to power; but when Orbiana was given the title of Augusta, Julia Mammaea's jealousy was savagely aroused. Orbiana's father was put to death and she herself exiled to Africa. Alexander was forced to submit to his mother's will, his protests going unheeded.

He was indeed a very gentle person, more concerned with the arts of peace than with the cruelty of war. Deeply religious, he began each day with prayers in his private chapel, where he placed statues of his favourite gods and the great men of the past. Included among them was a statue of Christ. Just under 200 years had passed since the Crucifixion and the followers of the new religion were still looked upon with suspicion, but the gentle Alexander found something appealing in the new doctrine. He relaxed some of the laws against Christians and it was said that he at one time wanted to build a temple in honour of Christ. He refrained only because the auspices showed that if this were done the old gods would fall into neglect and all men would follow the new faith.

Later, and perhaps reluctantly, he led his armies in the field. His legions were among the best equipped, best armed and best paid in the army's history, for he believed that soldiers would be obedient if they were treated well, equipped efficiently and paid generously. But he was no soldier. He led an army against the Persians and after initial setbacks finally defeated their king Ardeshir (Ataxerxes), but he came out of the campaign with his reputation tarnished. He had divided the forces into three divisions, leading one of these himself. This division came tardily into the battle after the other two had suffered murderous casualties, and his troops were to remember this incident with contempt and resentment. After his success in the East, he returned to Rome to enjoy a Triumph during which he was hailed as *Persicus Maximus*, a title which his troops must have heard with wry amusement. His generals won many victories in North Africa, Illyria and Armenia. New lands were brought into the Empire and allotted to time-expired soldiers, so that the frontiers might be guarded by trained men with a proprietary interest in the lands under their protection.

In spite of his personal virtues, Alexander's Principate was very different in character from the quasi-republican concept of Augustus or Vespasian and much closer to the idea of an Eastern monarchy. Indeed, his friends openly referred to him as king, and though he declined to accept the title of *Dominus* (the name given by a slave to his owner), the fact that it was offered shows what was in men's minds, and how the Emperor was increasingly seen as the owner and master of his people.

In 235, when he was twenty-seven, there was fighting on the western frontiers, where the German tribes had broken into Gaul, and Alexander led an army in person to repel them. Among the troops was one Caius Julius Maximinus, who had served under Septimius Severus; a peasant of barbarian descent, he had joined the army as a cavalryman. Severus had first noticed him during the games that had been organised for

Geta's birthday and had been impressed by his immense
stature and strength. The old emperor had spurred his horse
to a trot and bade Maximinus follow on foot. To Severus's
delight, the powerful Maximinus easily outran the horse. He
is said to have been over 8ft tall. It was rumoured that he
could consume 60 pints of wine and 40lb of meat a day, and
that he wore his wife's bracelet as a ring! Under Caracalla he
was promoted Centurion. Then, because of his prowess with
women, at least equal to his prowess at table, Elagabalus had
advanced him to the post of Tribune, and Alexander later
promoted him to senatorial rank.

By the time that Alexander marched to the Rhine, Maximinus was officer in charge of training of the newly enlisted.
His personal strength and his reputation in battle made him
successful in handling recruits and immensely popular with
the troops. They were less impressed by Alexander, for they
could not take seriously a leader who for too long had been
his mother's darling; nor could they easily forget that his
victories in the east had been won after disasters to which his
own vacillation, and perhaps cowardice, had contributed.
They remembered their dead companions, and their camps
buzzed with discontent, which hardened into a plot. Finally,
in March 235, the recruits hailed their beloved Maximinus as
emperor during a parade. Although he at first protested,
perhaps as a matter of form, he at length accepted their acclamations and so became Maximinus Augustus. A troop of
soldiers was speedily despatched to Alexander's camp, where
they slew the young Emperor and his mother in his tent, and
also slaughtered most of his friends and favourites. Those who
escaped were hunted down and slain. So ended the dynasty of
Bassianus the Syrian, which, largely through the resolution of
its womenfolk, had held power in Rome for nearly forty years.

All pretence that the title of Emperor was bestowed by the
Senate and people was now at an end. Sovereignty lay with the
sword. Maximinus saw no need to visit Rome nor to have his
appointment ratified by the surviving institutions of the now
defunct Republic. He led his troops forthwith against the
Germans, pursuing the only business he knew, the business of

war. He remained always a fighting soldier rather than a general, gaining his victories by feats of physical courage rather than by carefully planning his campaigns. He concluded the German war, assumed the title of *Germanicus*, and fought further campaigns along the Danube against the Dacians and the Sarmatians.

He brought to political affairs the same brutality that he had shown in battle; he was no respecter of persons and men of consular rank who opposed him were exiled or put to death. Remembering his own peasant origins, he went out of his way to humiliate and oppress the old aristocracy of Rome.

Then, in 238, there was an uprising in Libya. A harsh Procurator had been laying heavy taxes upon the local nobles. Some of the younger men from the old Carthaginian families organised a revolt, arming their servants with clubs and axes. Their ragamuffin army rose and assassinated the tyrannous official. Appalled by what they had done, the leaders knew that they had swiftly to throw a cloak of legality over their violent actions. The local governor, Gordian, was a man of nearly eighty who had spent a lifetime of service to the State. With their armed followers the young nobles went to his house, brushed aside the guards in the courtyard, and burst in with drawn swords to find the old man resting on a couch. They dressed him in a purple robe, hailing him as Augustus. He threw himself on his knees before them, pleading for his life, for their swords and the rude weapons of their followers convinced him that they had come to slay him, after first mocking him with the title of emperor. But in a formal speech they boasted that they had struck down the Procurator, who had been a servant of Maximinus the tyrant, and again offered him the purple which, after some pretence of unwillingness, he accepted. He was acclaimed throughout Libya and to this day mutilated inscriptions can be seen there from which the name and titles of Maximinus have been jubilantly erased. Statues of Gordian were set up and he was given the added title of *Africanus*. His son, also named Gordian, was made his colleague.

He set up his capital in Carthage, which briefly became a second Rome. To Rome itself he sent many letters addressed to all the leading citizens, condemning the brutality of Maximinus, and promising that all who had been unjustly convicted would be granted fresh trials, and that those whom Maximinus had exiled would be recalled. In all this he showed himself more sagacious than Maximinus, who had thought only of military action, and who did not once visit Rome after becoming Emperor.

Aristocratic Rome, whose resentment against the upstart Emperor had never been quenched, welcomed Gordian's approaches. To secure his position there, he sent a mission from Carthage to assassinate Vitalianus, Prefect of the Praetorians and a follower of Maximinus. The murder was successfully carried out, and the people of Rome, accustomed to the ruthlessness of Maximinus, assumed that it was his men who had slain Vitalianus. There was a spontaneous upsurge of anger against Maximinus, the mob rose, his soldiers were defeated, his monuments defaced, and crowds thronged the streets cheering the name of Gordian.

In Carthage Gordian was paying off old scores. The Governor of Numidia, Capellianus, was a follower of Maximinus and a man with whom Gordian had quarrelled before. With his new authority as Emperor, he sent one of his own men to replace him; but Capellianus did not wait to be superseded and marched his troops against Carthage, where Gordian's followers, led by his son, hurriedly and ineffectively armed the citizens. But the troops of Capellianus soon disposed of them, killing the younger Gordian, and the elder Gordian (who had enjoyed the name of Caesar for three brief weeks) hanged himself; and the soldiers of Capellianus roamed the bloody streets of Carthage, pillaging and looting.

The Senate, hearing of the disaster, was shocked. Its members had unwillingly tolerated the rule of Maximinus, the peasant, and had been overjoyed that once more a Senator, Gordian, should wield the authority of the Caesars. With Gordian dead, they assembled with particular solemnity in the temple of Jupiter on the Capitoline Hill to choose a successor.

After several votes they finally elected two of their number as joint emperors. One, Pupienus, was an experienced soldier; the other, Balbinus, had been a provincial governor and had twice held the office of Consul. Both were proclaimed Augustus and each was invested with the full authority of an emperor.

The people of Rome, however, broke into tumult when they heard the decision: Pupienus was unpopular with the citizens, and, moreover, many had been deeply moved by Gordian's rising against the tyrant Maximinus. All, therefore, wanted the Empire to pass to an heir of Gordian. Mobs blocked the roads round the temple and broke into open riot. Armed with sticks and stones they besieged the Senate, threatening the two new emperors. Balbinus and Pupienus hastily formed a bodyguard of young men, who, with swords drawn, faced the mob; but they were met by a shower of stones and had to retreat. The people clearly had to be placated. In Rome there was a thirteen year old boy who was the grandson of Gordian. Balbinus and Pupienus announced that they would make him their heir. Their messengers found him playing happily in his garden, and he was brought (no doubt bewildered) to the Senate, which formally bestowed upon him the name of Caesar, clad him in purple, and sent him forth on the shoulders of a tall man so that all might see him. The crowd, mollified, permitted Balbinus and Pupienus to enter the house of the Caesars.

News of these events reached Maximinus, who was still with his armies in the provinces. He became quite hysterical with rage. After the first outburst of anger he decided to march on Rome, crossing into Italy with his troops in the summer of 238, and laying siege to the city of Aquileia, where the citizens stoutly defied him. The women of Aquileia were as resolute as the men and cut off their hair to make bowstrings. Maximinus and his son (a youth of great beauty and fine presence, who had taken the name of Caesar) sent envoys to the city in vain. The citizens repelled all attacks, using burning sulphur and wreaking havoc among the troops of Maximinus. Finally, the demoralised troops decided to forsake their giant emperor. He and his son were slaughtered in their tent; their heads were stuck on poles and carried triumphantly from the camp.

Balbinus and Pupienus never truly gained the popularity of the people, whose loyalties were directed only to the boy Gordian. There followed a period of unrest and disorder. The two Emperors recruited a German bodyguard to secure the palace against the hostile people, an action resented by the Praetorian Guard, whose power and influence depended upon their position as custodians of the Caesars. They resolved to put an end to the troubles, choosing a day when most people were attending the theatre and when the two Emperors were virtually alone in the palace. They went first to the apartments of Pupienus, who was undefended, the German bodyguard being with Balbinus. Pupienus sent an urgent plea for help, but Balbinus, suspecting a trick, refused to send the guard. Eventually the Praetorians dragged the two Emperors from the palace and, when the German troops followed in pursuit, slaughtered them both, leaving the bloody corpses sprawling in the streets of Rome.

The Praetorian Guard, their power thus bloodily renewed, acclaimed Gordian as the sole Augustus. The new emperor being just a boy, however, he became the mere titular head of the Empire and other men ruled in his name.

Three years after his succession (when he was about sixteen years old) he married Tranquillina, the daughter of a most able officer named Timesthiseus. The latter took the post of Prefect of the Praetorian Guard and with it all effective power in the State. Fortunately for Rome he was both skilful and just. There followed a period of tranquillity in the city and of military successes on the frontiers. Unrest in Africa, two years after Gordian's succession, was quickly and effectively suppressed. Then the Persians, under their king Sapor, crossed the Euphrates and advanced upon the Roman city of Antioch. The young Emperor marched with a vast army, led by his father-in-law Timesthiseus, into Moesia and so southwards into Thrace. There his armies drove out invading tribesmen who, taking advantage of Rome's difficulties with her ancient enemies, the Persians, had overrun the frontiers of the empire.

Gordian's victorious legions continued their march into Asia. For a lad in his teens it must have been a brave sight to see the long columns of armed men, their helmets and weapons glittering in the southern sun, advancing along the dusty roads of Asia in his name. They advanced across Turkey and so into Syria until they came to the threatened city of Antioch, where they routed the armies of Sapor and expelled the proud Persian garrisons from the many cities they had occupied. Timesthiseus was now at the height of his powers. The Senate, in their congratulatory message, greeted him as 'The Father of Emperors, Prefect of the Guard and of all the City, Guardian of the Empire'. But such felicity could not last in the turbulent environment of the third century.

Among the officers with the Roman armies in Persia was an Arab named Marcus Julius Philipus—a burly, bearded man who had prospered in his army career but now had ambitions beyond mere military rank. Two men stood between him and the achievement of these ambitions—the nineteen-year-old emperor, darling of the army, and the mature and battle-trained Timesthiseus. The latter fell ill, possibly with dysentery, then grew worse. Some say that Philip interfered with the doctors' treatment. Timesthiseus died and so the post of Prefect of the Praetorian Guard fell suddenly vacant. It was vital to fill the vacancy with a man able to bring the war to a successful conclusion. So Philip the Arab was appointed Prefect and took over command of the armies.

When, nearly fifty years earlier, the Praetorian Guard had viciously murdered Pertinax, they had found a new role. No longer the personal protectors of the emperors, they had become a brutal power that made and unmade them. Now Philip was to use his position as their Prefect to win the imperial titles for himself. The troops, contrasting his mature ability with the youth of Gordian, were quick to proclaim him Caesar Augustus, at first as the colleague of Gordian. The nineteen year old lad, who had held nominal power since he was thirteen, was then bluntly told that he was no longer to share the empire with Philip. Gordian pleaded to be allowed to retain the name of Caesar, with some authority in the State, but this was denied him. Then, pathetically, he asked to be appointed Prefect of the Praetorians. This also was refused. Stripped of all power, Gordian begged at least to be allowed to live, but this final plea was spurned and he was callously butchered, by the army which had once adored him.

The year was 244. Philip, made a satisfactory peace with the Persians and returned to Rome to take possession of his imperial office. After the Syrian dynasty of Bassianus, and after the assumption of power by the Thracian Maximinus, no one thought it strange that an Arab should now sit on the curule chair of the Caesars.

During Philip's reign Rome was in holiday mood. The traditional date for her foundation was 753 BC and 248 was her thousandth anniversary. Spectacles and games, surpassing all those of former ages, were held. The citizens of Rome thronged to see beasts from every corner of the earth displayed or slaughtered for their delight. There were elks, strange deer from the wintry lands of the North, giraffes and a single rhinoceros, wild asses, lions, tigers, leopards, elephants and hyenas. Most of these had been gathered by poor Gordian in anticipation of his Persian triumph. The fickle people of Rome now thronged to see the same animals dedicated by the Arabian soldier who had slain their one-time hero.

The year before, Philip had bestowed the title of Augustus upon his son, also named Philip, and father and son presided over the games as Consuls. The coins of both reflect the joy which filled the City during the anniversary. One shows the she-wolf suckling Romulus and Remus, another bears the proud words *Romae Aeternae*, 'To Eternal Rome'; while others have such slogans as 'The Safety of the world', 'The Imperial Tranquillity', 'The Hope of the Fortunate Globe' and 'The Loyalty of the Soldiers'. Like many political slogans before and since they expressed aspirations rather than fact. For Philip the Arab there was little tranquillity and less loyalty. During the very year of the celebrations, when, crowned with laurel, he presided at the games or sat proudly in the Senate as Caesar, Augustus, The Dutiful, The Fortunate, the provinces stirred with unrest. His own success had shown how any ambitious soldier could seize the house of the Caesars on the Palatine hill and live at ease as ruler of the world. His own achievements provided the precedent for those who were to destroy him.

Somewhere, and no one knows where, a man named Marcus Silbannacus declared himself Caesar Augustus. The only surviving evidence of his existence is a single coin in the British Museum, which shows him wearing the radiate crown of an emperor. No man knows what stories of brief victory and sudden defeat lie behind this tiny and unique monument.

Philip sent his brother Priscus to govern Syria. Only fifteen years before, Syria had (as we have seen) been the cradle of emperors; so, when Priscus proved an arrogant and oppressive governor, the proud Syrians did not bear his tyranny patiently. A man named Marcus Fulvius Rufus Jotapianus, who claimed to be a descendant of Alexander Severus, led the garrison in a successful revolt against the hated governor, and the jubilant troops proclaimed Jotapian Emperor. They marched northwards past Antioch into Cappadocia. They were far from Rome itself but their leader was Emperor and they briefly tasted the sweet fruit of victory. But their success was as fragile as their loyalty: somewhere in Asia, they turned on Jotapian, a severe, thin-faced man with the stern eyes of a fighting commander, and murdered him.

In Upper Moesia a young soldier named Marinus Pacatianus saw no reason why he should not wear the purple so he added the names Tiberius Claudius to his own, and proclaimed himself Augustus. (Was he interested in history? It was just 200 years earlier that the stammering Claudius was proving himself an able and popular ruler.) But the troops who had supported him turned against him and slew him.

Among Philip's senior officers was a man named Decius, who had been born some forty-seven years earlier in the province of Pannonia. He had had a distinguished career and had been appointed to the rank of Senator. Ten years earlier, during the reign of Alexander Severus, he had been governor of Lower Moesia, and had quietly continued to administer the province throughout the troubled days of Maximinus. Although not Roman by birth, he seems to have looked back with understanding to former ages when Roman virtues prevailed, and devotedly worshipped the ancient gods of Rome.

For Philip, he was clearly the right man to calm the troubled land of Moesia, the centre of Pacatian's unsuccessful but dangerous usurpation; and there Philip sent him. Decius was successful, gaining the full confidence of the soldiers, who rejoiced to have such a stalwart figure as their leader; but by now the tradition that each army group declared its leader to be Emperor was well established. The soldiers accordingly acclaimed Decius as Caesar Augustus. At first he refused the dangerous honour, but when the soldiers offered him the stark alternative of acceptance or death, he reluctantly submitted. The exultant soldiers demanded that he should lead them to Rome to take up his high office. So in 249 the legions of Moesia marched westwards into what is now Yugoslavia, and along the shores of the Adriatic Sea into the northern plains of Italy.

Philip the Arab, knowing the prowess of Decius, realised that this was a very different matter from the pathetic usurpations of Jotapian, Silbannacus and Pacatian. He mustered a great army and, accompanied by his son, led his troops against the legions of Decius on the plains of northern Italy, close to the city of Verona. Philip fought with desperate resolution and the action was not broken off until both he and his son lay dead on the field of battle.

Decius, though himself a provincial, strove to restore the style and virtues of ancient Rome. Upon his son Etruscus he bestowed the name and rank of Caesar and revived for him the ancient title of *Princeps Juventutis*, leader of the youth. His wife Etruscilla came from an aristocratic Italian family, and coins were struck with her portrait, proclaiming the traditional virtues of Rome. His own coins demonstrated his interest in the past, bearing as they did portraits of former emperors, from Augustus to Alexander Severus.

He decided that one method of reviving the purity and splendour of former ages was to suppress the religions and superstitions that had invaded Rome from the eastern provinces. The reign of Elagabalus had shown what depravity such religions could foster. Among the new cults was Christianity, whose inflexible monotheism had come into sharp conflict with the loyal worship of Rome and Augustus. Earlier emperors had sought to destroy it, but later emperors had grown more tolerant, and the number of Christians was now large and their religion no longer clandestine. Philip the Arab, Decius's predecessor, had actively sympathised with the new faith, but Decius reintroduced harsh penalties against it, and the persecution that began in 250 was as cruel as any which had preceded it. For over a year the Christians in Rome were prevented from electing a new Bishop; and the throne of St Peter's successors, which was already acquiring a dominating influence in the Christian world, long lay vacant. It was said that Decius would sooner tolerate a rival for the Empire than a Bishop in Rome.

In the second year of his reign the Goths attacked the northern frontiers in force. Decius buckled on his armour and with his son Etruscus advanced to meet the threat. In Rome he left his younger son Hostilian, who now bore the rank of Caesar. The Goths were formidable fighters, but the Roman army was still an effective instrument and once more it had a fighting commander. They were victorious but Decius and Etruscus both died during the campaign. Some say they died in battle against the Goths; others that they were the victims of treachery at the hands of an ambitious officer named Trebonianus Gallus. What is certain is that Gallus took the title of Augustus and reigned for two and a half years. He could not disregard Decius's young son Hostilian, whom he appointed joint emperor with the equal rank of Augustus. The boy did not live long to enjoy his new honour, but died shortly afterwards of the plague which was sweeping through Europe.

Meanwhile Gallus made peace with the Goths, in a manner so damaging to the majesty of Rome that it added weight to the stories that, in league with them, he had plotted the death of Decius. We do not know his origins and his brief reign tells us little about him as a person, though much about the desperate state of the empire. The Goths broke the peace within a year and again invaded Moesia. There the governor, an African named Aemilianus, stoutly withstood them. In accordance with what was becoming standard practice, his soldiers hailed him as Augustus, and he marched on Italy, much as Decius had done four years earlier, boasting that he would drive out all the barbarians. Gallus called to his aid Licinius Valerianus, a sixty-year-old Roman aristocrat who had long served the State, having held the office of Censor under Decius, and ordered him to march against Aemilian with the garrisons of the Rhine. The fact that this vital frontier had to be stripped of its legions showed how constant usurpation by military commanders was tearing apart the tattered fabric of the Empire.

Valerian marched southwards but before he reached Italy news came of the death of Gallus at Verona. Valerian's troops, keyed up to play a part in deciding the fate of emperors, were unwilling to return to their garrison duties on the Rhine with no blow struck. Instead they declared Valerian emperor and continued their march into Italy. Thus, when Aemilian's troops turned and murdered him in 253, Valerian was left as the sole Emperor of Rome. He reigned for four years and the Empire, though it was beset by massive difficulties, enjoyed a brief period of stable government. The state was no longer at the mercy of popular tumult or military threat, and again had an Emperor who was himself a Roman. The Senate ratified the appointment of Valerian with grateful relief.

Valerian knew that any successful army commander was now a potential rival, while unsuccessful commanders were a threat to the security of the beleaguered empire. His solution was to appoint his son Gallienus as Augustus and co-emperor, placing him in command of the Rhine garrisons. He gave another military command to his elder son, Valerian, who received the lesser rank of Caesar. Having thus secured his position in the provinces through the ties of blood, he remained in Rome seeking to revive the revered standards of

I

the early Empire. He was cast in the mould of the great
Emperors of the past and his reputation stood high. That his
appointment had been made by the Senate renewed something of the latter's sovereign powers. The auguries were fair
and it seemed that tranquillity and prosperity were to return.
But three years after his accession the Persians attacked. Under
their great king, Sapor, they crossed the frontier and overwhelmed many of the garrisons.

Valerian, his age notwithstanding, led an army against them
to defend the line of the Euphrates. He advanced across that
river and the opposing armies met near the city of Odessa; the
Roman legions were surrounded and, though they made a
brave attempt to cut their way out of the trap, were driven
back with great slaughter. After Valerian had in vain offered
the Persians a huge ransom, they were compelled into ignom-
inious surrender and Valerian himself was made captive. For
Rome, this was a unique and humiliating tragedy: never
before had the sacred person of an Augustus been held prisoner
by a foreign foe.

Sapor led Valerian in triumph through Persia, loaded with
chains, dressed in imperial purple, as a demonstration of the
supremacy of Persian arms. Thereafter, whenever Sapor
mounted his horse, Valerian was forced to kneel as a mounting block. Nor was this all. After Valerian died it is said that
Sapor had his body stuffed and used it in the same way.

In Rome, news of Valerian's capture was received with
horror; but his foresight in appointing Gallienus as his co-
emperor ensured a peaceful succession. She was, however,
struck by almost every other type of disaster: the plague in
which young Hostilian had died raged intermittently for years;
the spectres of war and famine haunted the Empire; and
there were revolts in the provinces.

In the East, after the disgrace of Valerian's capture, the
defeated legions bravely rallied under the Prefect of the
Praetorian Guard, Ballista, and a fighting general named
Fulvius Julius Macrianus. The latter, perhaps to enhance the
legions' sense of purpose, declared his two sons Macrianus and
Quietus Emperors, and once more attacked the armies of

Sapor, throwing them back across the Euphrates. Then Macrianus led his army northwards into Europe, but in Illyria was confronted by troops loyal to Gallienus, and killed in the fighting.

The reign of Gallienus opened with success: he drove back the Germans who had invaded Gaul, and put down a revolt in Pannonia. But in Rome he revived the vices rather than the virtues of former days. It was said that he would enquire more eagerly about banquets and entertainments than affairs of state. Soon the whole Empire was in disarray. Rome's vast army was by constant civil war destroying both itself and the complex social and fiscal structure that supported it. To obtain the title of Augustus for their commanders, legion fought with legion and the international Roman state began to vanquish itself as efficiently as it had once conquered others. The Germans crossed Gaul, breaking into Italy and Spain. Dacia, won by the great Trajan, was lost. The Goths overran all Greece and Macedonia. Barbarians sailed from the Black Sea to the Danube, and Illyria was invaded. Region after region came under the fleeting rule of local emperors, each calling himself Augustus, the Dutiful, the Fortunate, but whose brief and selfish triumphs belied the names they bore. It was during the reign of Gallienus that there marched across the world scene that ruffianly procession of emperors known to history as the Thirty Tyrants. So confused are the events that even the number is in doubt. Some few achieved greatness but most were bandits, squandering the power of Rome to purchase an ephemeral and meaningless glory.

We have already met the two sons of Macrianus: one was slain in Illyria, the other, Quietus, at Emesa. A man named Ingenuus was now acclaimed Augustus by the legions in Moesia, but Gallienus ordered Postumus, who had been promoted to the command of the Rhine army by Valerian, to crush him, which he did.

The Empire was now suffering repeated blows. The first invaders were the Franks, warlike ancestors of the French nation. They broke through the frontier and, crossing Gaul, passed the Pyrenees into Spain, which they harried and looted, before crossing into Africa and ravaging the provinces there. Next, the Alemanni crossed the Danube and marched into northern Italy. There was no time for Gallienus to move south from the Rhine, but in the danger that threatened there was a flash of the old Roman virtues. The Senate called out the Praetorian Guard, and reinforced it with troops hastily recruited from the citizens of Rome. The reputation of the Roman legions was still high—more powerful than the pathetic weapons of this improvised army—and the Alemanni retreated.

Meanwhile Postumus and his armies stood firm on the Rhine. The peoples of Gaul, who had suffered such frequent invasions, once more began to feel secure behind the firm shield of Postumus, as constant in peace as he was courageous in war. Britain, too, benefited. With the Rhine securely guarded, the nations beyond that river, who had already begun to raid the province by sea, were given pause. Britain had escaped the continental curse of civil wars. Her towns were still orderly and the villas flourishing. True, the Picts had raided from the north, but three legions still garrisoned the province and Roman life continued. From overseas the Britons heard news of continued disasters; how Gallienus had surrendered Pannonia to a Germanic king whose daughter, Pipa, he had disgracefully taken as his mistress. The tough bearded figure of Postumus, whose strong army guarded the west, seemed a worthier embodiment of imperial power than the aristocratic but ineffective Gallienus.

In 259 Postumus declared himself Augustus, but did not think it necessary to march on Rome. He was content to leave Gallienus the luxury of the capital, scribbling poetry, taking a woman after dinner as another man might munch an apple for dessert, while he himself ruled the three Atlantic provinces of Spain, Gaul and Britain. He defeated Gallienus's ineffective attempts to remove him and for nearly ten years the West prospered under his firm rule. His coins, which are plentiful in Britain, tell us something of his purpose. One shows him in armour on the obverse, and, on the reverse, Hercules overcoming the wild horses. On other coins Hercules reoccurs, always the symbol of strength and endurance. One shows Postumus wearing the hero's lion-skin cloak, and another depicts Hercules as 'The Bringer of Peace'—showing that Postumus considered his legions as guardians of the citizens and not as mere instruments of personal power.

For all his virtues, however, his life ended violently. In 268 Laelianus (another of the thirty tyrants) led an armed rebellion against him on the Rhine frontier. Postumus swiftly defeated and slew him, capturing his base, the town of Moguntiacum (Mainz). The troops moved in to sack the city and to enjoy a few days of raping and looting, but Postumus (Hercules, 'The Bringer of Peace') would have none of this. Frustrated and forgetting in their blood-lust his achievements and their own loyalty, his own troops murdered him.

Postumus did much to shape the future. He revived the concept of the emperor as a protector, showed that resolution could still hold back the barbarians and, most important, demonstrated that the western Empire could survive as a separate entity and could be most effectively governed by a local emperor. The formal division of the empire into east and west was to follow.

In the same year the armies of Illyria invaded northern Italy to overthrow Gallienus, now notorious for his depravity. Among their officers were two men named Claudius and Aurelianus. Gallienus assembled his legions, and the armies confronted one another near Milan. At the siege of that city Gallienus, now fifty years old, was murdered by the rebels and his wife perished with him. Claudius was immediately proclaimed Caesar Augustus and reigned for two triumphant years. An Illyrian by birth, he had been a soldier from his youth, developing great physical strength. He was a brilliant general and had been promoted both by Decius and Valerian.

The empire to which he succeeded was perilously beset. First he had to crush a rebellion by Aureolus, an Illyrian who had been in command of Gallienus's cavalry. Claudius defeated him at a battle for a river crossing, where Aureolus was slain. Meanwhile the Goths, perceiving the Empire's weakness, mustered a huge army, drawn from their numerous tribes.

Claudius, though greatly outnumbered, brilliantly defeated them, driving them out of Moesia and the other provinces they had invaded. Many of the defeated Goths were settled as Treaty Troops within the empire, and it seemed that the perennial barbarian threat had been overcome. Claudius took the name of Gothicus, conqueror of the Goths. But plague succeeded where battle had failed. The Gothic soldiers had brought a pestilence with them, of which Claudius died in 276, honoured and beloved. His biographer wrote that he had the manhood of Trajan, the virtue of Antoninus and the moderation of Augustus. Had he lived he might have changed the course of history by restoring Rome's failing fortunes.

Meantime in the plague-stricken western Empire the sorry tale of chaos and usurpation continued. After Postumus's death a man named Marius, who had started life as a blacksmith, proclaimed himself Caesar Augustus in the West. His triumph was short-lived, for he was murdered three days later, some say with a sword of his own forging. Thereupon a fellow officer, Victorinus, was proclaimed Emperor in his stead. He had been one of Postumus's aides but proved an unworthy successor, the only memorial he left being a squalid reputation as a womaniser. He exploited his authority to seduce the wives of his soldiers and officers, and was finally murdered at Cologne by an outraged husband. During his brief reign of some two years the western Empire was nearly destroyed. Spain broke free from his rule and later he faced troubles in Gaul—from which he was saved by the assassin's weapon!

Victorinus had appointed as governor of Aquitaine a man named Esuvius Tetricus who, on the death of Victorinus, was declared Augustus. By now the dominions he inherited had shrunk to Gaul and Britain. Tetricus was a precursor of those monarchs in the narrow territories of medieval kingdoms.

When Claudius Gothicus died in 270, he was succeeded in Rome by Aurelian, that other Illyrian officer, who had been his confederate in the rising against Gallienus. Claudius had left a younger brother Quintillus, who was proclaimed emperor at Aquileia, but when Aurelian marched against him his troops deserted him and Quintillus committed suicide.

Although Aurelian was already sixty-three, his vigour and ability remained undiminished. He had many military exploits to his credit, and on one campaign he was said to have killed forty-eight of the enemy. He had defeated the Franks and had campaigned against the Persians. He was one of Rome's greatest generals and a born leader, demanding from each of his troops a soldier's obedience but not the subservience of a slave. Resolved to restore the unity of the Empire, he set out for Gaul in 273 to put an end to the usurpation of Tetricus, and such was his reputation that Tetricus yielded peaceably. Aurelian, as magnanimous as he was valiant, treated Tetricus with honour, giving him an official post in Italy, though insisting that he march in his Triumph as a captive.

Except for Dacia, he restored all the lost provinces of the Empire. In the east, the city of Palmyra had established its own dominion over many of the neighbouring provinces. Aurelian liberated them, and Queen Zenobia of Palmyra was led as a captive, like Tetricus, at his Triumph in Rome, with prisoners from all the barbarian tribes whom Aurelian had defeated.

Aurelian now resolved to humble the Persians and to re-establish the frontiers of the East. So he assembled a great army and marched to Byzantium, which city was to be the base for his campaign. But with advancing years (he was now sixty-eight) he had grown less tolerant and was inflicting harsh punishments on all who opposed him, earning the hatred of many. One of his secretaries, a freedman named Eros, was among those who bore him a grudge. Eros circulated a list of names which, he said, were those of men whom Aurelian had decided to execute, and, with the support of those who believed themselves to be in peril, assassinated Aurelian during his march south from Byzantium in 275.

The armies of Illyria, whose officers had now twice provided the Empire with able rulers, sent dutiful messages to the Senate undertaking to follow any emperor that body might choose. The Senate elected a seventy-five-year-old Roman named Tacitus, who claimed descent from the great historian. He revived the religious aspects of his office, placed his personal wealth at the disposal of the state, dressed without ostentation, and exercised moderation in all that he did. After introducing reforms in Rome, he led an army into Thrace to oppose an invasion of the Goths, who were once more on the move. The rigours of the campaign, however, were too much for the old man, and he died in Cappadocia in Asia in April 276.

His brother, Flavianus, proclaimed himself Caesar Augustus and was recognised by the Senate, but the armies of the East preferred Probus, one of Aurelian's generals. They proclaimed him Emperor and in the ensuing civil war, Flavianus was murdered by his troops after a reign of little more than two months. Probus ruled wisely for six years, continuing the work of Aurelian. He was a native of Pannonia and his father had been a soldier before him. Singled out for his great strength, he had been promoted Tribune by Valerian, and Gallienus had also advanced him in his career. He was an excellent regimental officer, keeping a close eye on such everyday matters as the equipment, clothing and boots of his men. Under Aurelian he served in North Africa and Egypt, which province he restored to the authority of Rome. The Senate ratified his appointment, recalling his many successful campaigns, and he restored to that assembly its ancient rights to hear appeals, to appoint proconsuls, and to give final approval to his own enactments.

Having punished the murderers of Aurelian and secured the loyalty of all the armies in Europe, Probus set out for Gaul, which had again been invaded by the Germans. He drove the invaders back across the Rhine, built defensive works on the eastern bank and recruited some of the defeated Germans into the armies of Rome. He settled some of their leaders in Britain. Having reported his success to the Senate, he turned on the Vandals and Burgundians and defeated them.

Despite his high reputation, there were at least two attempts to usurp his authority. The first came from a rich man named Proculus, once a successful legionary commander, now living on vast estates near Genoa, part farmer, part brigand. He used to boast to his friends that he could transform 100 virgins into women in a fortnight! With a like unreality he proclaimed himself Caesar Augustus, but Probus quelled him with ease and contemptuously banished him. The second aspirant was Bonosus, a former centurion, who had been placed in charge of the Rhine armies after Probus's victories. Some said he was a Spaniard, some a Briton. He was a prodigious drinker and could drink German prisoners of war into garrulous and therefore informative inebriation. He was no doubt a splendid intelligence officer, but as guardian of the Rhine frontier he was a failure. The Germans regrouped, attacked, and burned many of the Roman galleys policing the river. In a desperate attempt to save himself from Probus's anger he declared himself Augustus at Cologne in 280. He retained his troops' loyalty and withstood Probus for longer than he either deserved or hoped. Finally defeated, he hanged himself. Remembering his heroic drinking, the troops grimly jested that the wine bottle had been finally hung up.

Probus, after a spectacular Triumph in Rome to celebrate his German victories, set out for the Persian frontier. He used to say that he looked forward to the time when, the frontiers secure and the provinces pacified, there would be no more soldiers. Arms would no longer be made, nor horses bred for war. Oxen would plough in peace and Roman law would everywhere prevail. On his march towards Persia in 282, he anticipated this golden age of peace. Planning to enlarge his native city of Sirmium in Illyria, he ordered his troops to lay aside their swords and to drain the marshes. Military tradition was too strong for the experiment to be a success. The soldiers first grumbled at their unaccustomed task, then mutinied, turned against Probus and murdered him, so ending his dream of peace.

The Praetorian Guards proclaimed their Prefect Marcus Aurelius Carus as Augustus. He continued the warlike plans of Probus and set out against the Persians, accompanied by his younger son Numerianus, leaving his elder son Carinus to rule in Rome with the rank of Caesar. Carus defeated the Persians, but was killed by lightning in 283 while still on campaign. Numerian, acclaimed in the field as Augustus, led the army by slow marches back to Europe, accompanied by a general named Diocletianus, who commanded his bodyguard. But Numerian was murdered in Thrace, some say by officers of the Praetorian Guard. Diocletian arrested and executed the murderers and himself took command of the army.

Meanwhile Numerian's brother Carinus had been proclaimed Augustus in Rome, though his authority was immediately challenged by Julianus, commander in Pannonia, who declared himself Augustus. Carinus defeated him near Verona in 285, however, and ruled as one of the most debauched of the emperors. An adulterer and glutton, a corrupter of youth and a homosexual, he filled the palace with a crew of pimps, procurers and prostitutes. His life, incidentally, disproves the theory that there is moral virtue in cold baths—for he always bathed in ice cold water!

Shortly after his accession, news came that Diocletian had been proclaimed Augustus by the army returning from the East. Carinus took the field, but his soldiers, preferring to serve the stern figure of Diocletian, murdered him. Diocletian now stood alone, sole master of the Empire, confidently facing the perils that beset him.

V · DIOCLETIAN TO THEODOSIVS

Recovery and Final Fall -
Fourth Century AD ·

Diocletian, greatest of the Illyrian soldier-emperors, was born in Dalmatia of a very ordinary family, and joined the army as a youth. A story was later told how he and a friend consulted the Druids when they were soldiering in Gaul. The Druids told them that one of them would become emperor 'once he had slain the boar'. Young Diocletian hopefully made boar-hunting his pastime, but, though he killed many, he remained a subordinate. Years later, however, he slew a man named Arius Aper (whose surname means 'the boar') and suddenly realised his imperial destiny. He was proclaimed Augustus by his troops at Chalcedon, immediately on the death of Numerian, in 284, when he was just under forty. He had close-cropped hair, a carefully trimmed beard and the stern brows and tight lips of a man of action. He had watched the Empire become the plaything of competing generals, and may have wondered why general after general had risked death in order to enjoy the ephemeral title of Augustus and the fatal name of Caesar. He seems to have concluded that the turmoil of the last decades paradoxically made a division of rule the only hope of unity. Personal ambition alone had not urged Postumus to take over Gaul, Britain and Spain; based on the Rhine, he knew he was better able to protect the western provinces than an Augustus enthroned remotely in Rome. Other usurpers had perhaps been guided by similar motives. The immensity of Rome's task, with the limited means of communication then available, makes it surprising that no earlier ruler had anticipated Diocletian's vision. Despite the well-organised system of imperial posts, the complex network of roads and the relays of horses stabled along the highways of Europe, it still took many days or weeks for news to come from the frontiers to the Augustus in Rome. He could not possibly react to events with the speed which the troubled times demanded. Many of the usurpers were perhaps fumbling towards a solution of this dilemma. Much was to be said for having men with imperial authority stationed on the Rhine, or in Pannonia, or ruling from the city of Palmyra on Rome's sensitive frontier with Persia. Diocletian's claim to fame is that he formalised this development. He also established a system whereby, on the death of an Emperor, his authority would pass peacefully to his successor, so that the end of each reign would not be the occasion for recurrent civil war.

First he took another soldier as a colleague, sharing with him the title of Augustus. He chose Valerius Maximianus, an Illyrian professional soldier like himself, appointing him co-emperor in 286. These two held equal power, but Diocletian marked his own seniority by taking the name of Jovius, after the father of gods and men, and bestowing on Maximianus the lesser name of Herculius, after Hercules, who, while more than human, was something less than divine.

Early in his reign economic disaster was added to the perils of invasion and plague. In Gaul gangs of poor peasants called the 'Bacaudae' roamed the countryside, with banditry their only occupation and robbery their only support. It was by a successful campaign against them that Maximianus had won Diocletian's esteem, and as Augustus he was given administration of the western provinces of Spain, Gaul and Britain, and the lands north of the Alps and west of the Danube. He was closer to his dominions than any man in Rome could have been and his reactions to events were so much the swifter and surer. Diocletian himself governed the eastern provinces with a like authority. The decisions of either were binding upon the other. The example of Postumus was now being put to good purpose. Victory once more hovered over the standards of the legions and the stern Roman peace was re-established, from the grey Atlantic to the warm waters of the Tigris and Euphrates, and from the northern moors of Britain to the hot plains of Africa.

The system worked, and in 293 Diocletian took steps to achieve his second purpose of an orderly succession. He and Maximianus each appointed a deputy with the name and rank of Caesar. On the death of an Augustus, he was to be succeeded by his Caesar, whose power would be already great and whom none could effectively challenge. The existence of four emperors, two senior and two junior, made possible a further devolution of local authority and closer surveillance of the furthest provinces. As Caesar in the west, Diocletian appointed Flavius Valerius Constantius, nicknamed *Chlorus* or 'the Pale', a man of aristocratic descent from Dardania. In the east, a second Caesar was appointed—Galerius Valerius Maximianus, who came from Dacia. Originally a shepherd, his ability, coupled with a certain ruthlessness, had brought him advancement in the army and now had won him an imperial rank. He claimed he was related to Claudius Gothicus. Diocletian fortified the mutual loyalty of the two Augusti and the two Caesars by marriage. Constantius was made to divorce his wife Helena, mother of his son, and marry Maximianus's stepdaughter Theodora. Galerius, too, divorced his wife and married Valeria, Diocletian's daughter. Thus the two Caesars became the sons-in-law of the two Augusti.

Diocletian's tetrarchy (the system of four rulers) won for the Empire a further 100 years of existence. Had it endured, Rome's rule and the unity she had imposed upon Europe might have survived much longer.

Like others who had sought a revival of ancient virtues, Diocletian and his colleagues were faced with the problem of the alien religions that had invaded the Empire from the east. Most ancient of these was the cult of Mithras, brought to Rome from Persia, some say by pirates captured during Pompey's Mediterranean campaign centuries before. It was the favoured religion of the Roman army. Expressed as a military metaphor, with the legions of light ranged on the side of righteousness and the legions of darkness supporting the adversary of the true god, it made a great appeal to the soldiers. Wherever there was a camp or barracks, there was a statue of Mithras and a place for his worship. On the remote frontier of Hadrian's Wall, in the busy trading city of London, in the garrison towns of Spain, along the embattled Rhine and Danube, statues and votive tablets, inscriptions and ruined buildings, provide evidence of the legions' earnest worship of their Lord of Light.

The second alien religion to flourish in Rome was Christianity. We have seen that there were probably Christians in Rome in the reign of Claudius, ten years or so after the Crucifixion. Paul's Epistles record that during his lifetime there were Christians in the imperial household. During the reigns of Claudius, Nero and later emperors, most of the secretaries and imperial officials were freedmen who had known the indignities that go with the ownership of one man's body by another; to such, the compassion of Christianity made an immediate appeal. Nero's savage slaughter of Christians, as scapegoats for the fire that had destroyed Rome, did not destroy the faith. The conflict between Christianity and the state arose from the Christians' obstinate refusal to break the first commandment. Rome allowed men to worship whatever gods they pleased, provided that they also gave worship to Rome and the Augustus. The sprinkling of a little incense upon an official altar, a polite bow to the spirit of the city and its emperor, were the least gestures owed by men to the state, whatever their philosophical or metaphysical beliefs. Officialdom could not understand the recalcitrance that denied the state this minimum courtesy, nor realise that the exclusive worship of the one true God lay at the very heart of the new faith.

By the time of Diocletian, Mithraism and Christianity had captured the minds of vast numbers of the citizens of the Empire. Broadly, the army followed Mithras and worshipped the sun, seeing their emperors as companions of the unconquered Sun God, while the civilian population, particularly in the great cities, followed Christ, believing that salvation lay in the love of each man for his neighbour and in the forgiveness of sins by God and man. To Diocletian the Mithras cult was acceptable, for it did not erode the unity of the Empire, its followers revering the emperor as the companion of their god and accepting his authority as quasi-divine. Not so the Christians, who were opposed utterly to the whole concept of state worship, who could accept no emperor as divine and who placed their God above and apart from the person of the Augustus.

Diocletian, therefore, began the last and probably the most savage of Rome's persecutions of the Christians. He issued a series of harsh edicts against the Church, the first in 303, and the persecution lasted for eight terrible years. Churches were demolished and copies of the Gospels destroyed; and Christians who would not recant were pursued and executed. These dark days furnished the first recorded martyrs in Britain —Aaron, Julian and Alban, of whom the last is the best known. He had helped a priest to escape pursuit and, when arrested, announced that he too had become a Christian. He refused to recant and was executed on the rising ground outside the city of Verulamium. On that low hill now stands the Cathedral Church of St Albans, whose altar, so tradition says, is built over the very spot of his martyrdom. The modern name of the city is his permanent memorial.

In the West Constantius Chlorus was responsible for carrying out the edict. It was said that he did so with moderation and that his own sympathies lay with the Christians. Because his son became the great champion of Christianity, perhaps these stories were invented afterwards. Certainly there was persecution in the West, where numerous churches were destroyed and where death came to many of the faithful. It was also said that initiative for the persecutions lay with

Galerius rather than Diocletian, for the latter had certainly shown some sympathy for the Christians during the early part of his reign. That, and the known ruthlessness of Galerius, add colour to the story.

During this time a series of dramatic events was taking place in Britain which indirectly were to have far-reaching effects upon the history of Rome and indeed upon the history of the world. Gaul and Britain were now suffering continual raids by pirates from the tribes dwelling east and north of the Rhine Estuary. Stout ships made swift landings along the northern shores of Gaul and the south-eastern shores of Britain. Villas were raided, buildings were burned, treasures looted, women raped and citizens enslaved. Chief among these raiders were the Saxons, who were later to overrun the island and to build their kingdoms on the ruins of the Roman province; but yet there was no question of permanent settlement, only sudden brutal raids. No one could tell where the square-rigged longboats would make their landings. The legions provided but poor defence, for no troops could march as swiftly as ships could sail. Frequently they arrived too late, to gaze helplessly on the smoke of a burning villa, to bury the dead and to comfort the survivors.

From the earliest times Rome had organised a British fleet, the *Classis Britannica*. To face the new danger Rome now re-established and strengthened the British fleet, which we have already seen under Agricola and Hadrian. It was now based partly upon Britain and partly upon Gessoriacum (Boulogne). The Romans were not great sailors, so to command the fleet they appointed a soldier from the very tribes who were carrying out the raids, a man named Carausius, a Menapian. The coins which he was later to mint show him as a tough bearded helmeted man, blunt of nose and strong of jaw.

For a while Rome's new tactics were successful and the British fleet was able to intercept the pirates at sea. But it began to be noticed that Carausius's fleet was attacking the pirates after the raids rather than before, confiscating their loot and transfering it to their own ships. The plunder was not returned to the owners, and Carausius grew rich with abundant booty. Wealth gave him power, and his fleet gave him total independence from the central authority of Rome. So Carausius was dismissed, but he laughed at the order and sailed to Britain with the squadron that lay at Boulogne. Secure behind the narrow seas, confident that no Continental legions could attack him while he controlled the Channel, he declared himself Augustus in 287, assuming imperial authority in Britain and Boulogne.

Carausius is the first recorded discoverer of Britain's destiny : that she is an island; that her shield is the sea; and that any ruler in Britain who commands those seas can safely defy any Continental military power—even one as mighty as imperial Rome. Carausius' discovery remained valid until the twentieth century when the invention of aircraft gave a new dimension to the art of war.

Carausius issued an abundant coinage from the mints of London and Colchester, inscribed with his proud title of Augustus. One at least bears the Capricorn badge of the Second Legion, which had been stationed in Britain since the conquest and which evidently supported him.

Britain was now virtually a sovereign state, though nominally still a province of the Empire. Her legions still marched behind their old standards, her cities still had their magistrates and prefects. But, isolated from the continent, she was learning how to live as an independent country.

It was now that nine maritime strongholds were built in south-east Britain; the ruins of many stand to this day, at Richborough, Pevensey, Lympne and elsewhere. These are known as the Saxon forts and were long considered to have been built later, to protect the coast against the Saxon invaders. But it is now believed that they were constructed by Carausius as a defence against attempts by the central government to invade his island and unseat him.

Maximianus, realising that his landlocked Continental armies were powerless against the island usurper, took no steps to put Carausius down. Indeed, to hide Rome's impotence, he officially recognised Carausius, who thus legally enjoyed the title he had arrogantly assumed. He ruled for five successful

K

years, secure in his island fortress, nominally representing the imperial authority of Rome. Then Rome withdrew her recognition and Constantius Chlorus, now Caesar in the West, marched against Gessoriacum and captured it. Though bereft of his base in Gaul, Carausius still reigned secure in Britain.

Among Carausius's followers was a man named Allectus, his financial adviser and second-in-command. Coveting imperial rank and encouraged by the fact that Carausius no longer enjoyed Rome's support, Allectus led a revolt in 293, killed Carausius, and took the title of Augustus himself. For three years he, too, ruled successfully in Britain. Like Carausius, he issued coins from the British mints and upon them he appears wearing the traditional laurel wreath of the Caesars. To honour the fleet, the guardian of his independence, Allectus struck a coin showing a warship—perhaps the first depiction of any unit of a British Fleet.

In 296, however, Constantius Chlorus decided to restore Britain to the Empire. He organised an expeditionary force in Gaul and assembled a great fleet at Gessoriacum. Thence the ships sailed in two divisions, one commanded by Constantius himself and the other by Asclepiodotus, Prefect of his Praetorian Guard. There was a dense fog in the Channel. Allectus's fleet and lookouts on the shore saw nothing of the warships as they moved silently over the waters. Asclepiodotus made an unopposed landing on the south coast, marched inland, and defeated the forces of Allectus in a fierce battle in Hampshire. Allectus himself died in the fighting.

Meantime Constantius landed at the port of Richborough, and rode at the head of his troops along Watling Street to London, which he cleared of the forces of the dead usurper. Two relics of the battle for London remain. When the foundations of London's County Hall were dug in the 1920s, the wreck of a Roman warship was found preserved in the Thames mud—almost certainly a unit of Allectus's fleet sunk in the fighting. Second, a gold medal, found in France, struck in honour of the victory, shows Constantius riding to the gates of London, while a figure representing the city kneels at his feet in gratitude. The inscription describes him as the man who restored to Britain the eternal light of Roman civilisation.

Also in 296 a soldier named Domitian proclaimed himself Augustus in Egypt and reigned briefly in Alexandria. In 297 the legions of Diocletian besieged him there, took the city, and put a bloody end to his fleeting glory.

In 306 Diocletian, now approaching sixty, put his new system to the final test: in failing health, he laid down his office, divesting himself of all power and retiring to his estates in Illyria. The ruins of his palace in Yugoslavia still stand, and the story of the old man, once the ruler of a great empire and commander of many glittering legions, peacefully growing cabbages in his quiet Adriatic garden is well-known.

He imposed the same decision upon his colleague Maximianus, who accepted the ruling with reluctance. So in the early summer of 306 the two Caesars peacefully succeeded. Constantius, fresh from his British victory, became Augustus in the West, while Galerius became Augustus in the East, occupying the imperial palace in Nicomedia. The tetrarchy continued and two new Caesars were appointed: in the West an experienced soldier named Flavius Valerius Severus, and in the East a young kinsman of Galerius named Galerius Valerius Maximinus. Both were the nominees of Galerius, who through them thus wielded greater power than Constantius, nominally the senior Augustus. To ensure Constantius's loyalty, Galerius arranged that Constantius's son by his first wife Helena, Constantine, should stay with him in Nicomedia, ostensibly an honoured guest but in truth a hostage.

Shortly after becoming Augustus, Constantius organised a second expedition into Britain in order to deal with the Picts, the painted tribesmen from the north, who had crossed Hadrian's Wall and were raiding far to the south. Before sailing, he sought Galerius's permission to take his son with him. Constantine, now more than thirty years old, had already distinguished himself in several campaigns and was immensely popular, but this popularity had aroused the suspicions of Galerius, who granted permission with the greatest reluctance. Constantine, fearing that the grudging permission might be withdrawn, left Nicomedia secretly by night and rode with all haste across Europe, accompanied by a small escort. He reached Gessoriacum just in time to join his father's expedition and sailed with him across the Channel.

It was a dramatic moment when Constantine stepped ashore, for Britain was to be the base from which he was later to seize power. To the armies of Britain he was to provide a dazzling and dangerous example, which his successors were frequently to follow. But for the present all was excitement and success. Father and son marched victoriously northwards, and defeated the marauding Picts. For Constantine, brought up in the east, everything was new : the long delights of lengthy summer days; the freshness of sudden rain; the lace of winter frost; the welcome warmth of centrally heated barracks, the more genial for the desolation of a northern November; the grass standing green in all seasons; the fat cattle and orchards heavy with crisp and reddened fruit.

Constantius restored the broken defences of Hadrian's Wall and modernised the important military centre of York. There he built a great multi-angular tower, much of which stands to this day; a sombre reminder of those days of peril and endeavour. Constantine helped his father in these tasks and learned much. His father, now approaching sixty, with the fatigue of many campaigns upon him, fell ill in York—military centre of the north. Constantine was with him when he died and York, for the second time, saw the solemn pomp of an Emperor's funeral.

The tetrarchy was not based upon heredity, so that his father's death gave Constantine no special rights, but so great was the glory of his father's name and so golden his own reputation, that the troops of Britain joyfully acclaimed him Caesar, which title he as joyfully accepted. He wrote formally to Galerius protesting that he himself had not usurped the purple but that his armies had insisted. Galerius, no doubt reluctantly, confirmed him in his title of Caesar, but marked his displeasure by elevating Severus to the rank of Augustus, and appointing Maxentius (son of Maximianus) first as *Princeps*, then, later in the same year, Caesar and then Augustus. One of the first acts of Maxentius was to invite his father to resume the title of Augustus and Maximianus, who had with reluctance obeyed Diocletian's directive to abdicate, eagerly complied. Faced with these events Constantine, realising that he might have to defend his new title, resolutely prepared his armies for war. He spent the next seven months in Britain, where five milestones referring to 'Constantine the Caesar' have been discovered, showing that he must have repaired the system of roads as part of his preparations.

Galerius was furious at the reappointment of Maximianus, who could now claim to be the senior Augustus. The recently appointed Augustus of the West, Severus, was ordered to march against Maximianus, but his troops had no stomach for the fight, and he was captured and put to death by the old Emperor. Constantine now crossed to the Continent and set up his headquarters at Trèves. He was now a figure of massive importance. Although Diocletian's tetrarchy was outwardly continuing, there was clearly going to be a brutal struggle for power. Realising this, Maximianus, in 307, visited Constantine in Gaul, almost as a suppliant, to seek an alliance, Constantine's assessment of his own power must have been reinforced by this approach. Recently a self-appointed Caesar whose authority depended upon the loyalty of a handful of troops in a remote island province, he was now being courted by one of the masters of the world. He offered the older man his full support and, as we shall see, long kept his word.

To give public form to the private alliance, Constantine divorced his wife, Minervina, who had recently borne him a son, Crispus. (History was repeating itself. Crispus, like Constantine, grew up in the knowledge that his mother was the victim of the harsh game of power.) Constantine then married Fausta, Maximianus's daughter, who later bore him three sons, each of whom was to wield the sceptre. Meanwhile Galerius decided to strike before the new alliance became effective. He marched out of the East and invaded Italy. No troops opposed his march on Rome, but in Rome itself Maxentius grimly awaited his coming. The city was well garrisoned and abundantly stocked to withstand a siege.

The armies of Galerius, their peaceful march over, took up their assault positions outside the walls. Rome beset by Roman armies demonstrated the final dissolution of the tetrarchy of Diocletian. But Galerius's soldiers had no appetite for battle, and fell an easy prey to Maxentius's agents, who tempted them with bribes and moved them to mutiny. Galerius, far from his base, could not afford to forfeit their loyalty and withdrew them from the siege. To match the promises of his enemies he allowed his men to plunder the countryside, and to take their fill of loot on their march back to the province of Pannonia.

Elated by his son's success, Maximianus returned to Rome, eager for power; but Maxentius was in no mood to share authority—even with his father. The two quarrelled, and Maximianus, with no foundation upon which to rebuild his authority, retreated disconsolately to Gaul and to the protection of his son-in-law Constantine. On the chessboard of Europe the pieces were moving towards stalemate. The two senior Augusti, Maximianus and Galerius, stood warily opposed, each recently rebuffed and neither capable of final victory. Galerius, having failed to find a military solution, decided that the two rivals should sit down together and talk. In 308 he called a conference at Carnuntum for which Diocletian was called out of his retirement. Round the conference table an attempt was made to re-establish some kind of order. After hard negotiations a settlement was reached.

The defeated Maximianus was to abdicate for the second time and his son, Maxentius, was declared an enemy of the state. Constantine, who had previously been granted the title of Augustus, had once more to be content with the rank of Caesar. This left Galerius in full command of the eastern Empire and the sole Augustus. To replace Constantine as Augustus of the West, Galerius promoted Licinius, one of his own officers. Another of his officers, Maximinus, remained Caesar in the East. His grip on the Empire was now complete. But the structure of government established at Carnuntum was inherently unstable. Both Constantine and Maximinus bitterly resented the appointment of Licinian as Augustus. He had not served in the junior position of Caesar; nor had he the experience of power which they possessed. Galerius bestowed upon both Constantine and Maximinus the flattering but worthless title of 'Son of the Emperor' (*Filius Augusti*). Neither found this empty designation acceptable and, in the following year, Galerius was compelled to grant to both Constantine and Maximinus the coveted designation of Augustus.

The Roman world now had four Augusti. This was not the orderly tetrarchy of Diocletian, a framework within which colleagues could work harmoniously together. The situation had grown from the conflict of four powerful men and the result was a perilous fragmentation of imperial authority.

Constantine remained loyal to his father-in-law Maximianus who, after the settlement of Carnuntum, was his honoured guest. Then in 311 Constantine marched with an army to the Rhine frontier, to defend his territories against the threat of another barbarian invasion. Maximianus, heedless alike of gratitude and of his son-in-law's military genius, made another bid for power. At the court of the absent Constantine he gained the adherence of a number of troops, and seized the imperial treasury at Arles. Constantine rushed his armies back to southern Gaul, partly by forced marches and partly by boat down the Rhône-Saône valley. Only a general of outstanding ability could have redeployed his forces so swiftly. Behind the curt phrases of history we have to see the marshalling of men and horses, the preparation of rations and forage, the planning of routes, the assembling of boats for the river journey and the posting of a strong rearguard on the Rhine.

Maximianus withdrew from Arles, and retreated south to Marseilles, where Constantine's armies pursued him. The city was taken by assault and Maximianus died. Some say that he took his own life, others that he was put to death by Constantine. After the fighting was over, Constantine sternly stamped out the embers of revolt. Terror was one of his weapons, and the chieftains of some of the tribal armies which had supported Maximianus were torn to pieces by wild beasts in the arena at Trèves for the delight of all loyal citizens and as an example to their fellows.

In the same year (311) Galerius, the tough and ruth-less soldier who for so long had wielded the chief power in the state, was stricken with a savage illness. His body, for so long dressed in the purple gown of authority, was invaded by pain and putrefaction. Worms consumed his flesh and maggots crawled over the once proud muscles. Memories of his victories, of the authority he had built with such ruthless skill, of his savage persecution of the Christians—all dissolved in agony. He died after a week of horror and Maximinus now became the senior Augustus.

Maxentius, though declared a public enemy at Carnuntum, continued to rule Italy and parts of North Africa. There in 311 Lucius Domitius Alexander, a local commander, saw in the political chaos of Europe an opportunity to declare him-self Augustus. His base was the ancient city of Carthage, but the armies of Maxentius swiftly defeated him, and, a forgotten man, he died defending his pathetic authority.

There were now three Augusti—Maximinus, Constantine and Licinius. If the system of Diocletian was to be restored, one had to be destroyed. Licinius had been a nominee of Galerius and, with the latter's death, his stature was notably diminished.

Constantine decided to make him his ally, knowing that if jointly they could put down Maximinus, he himself would emerge as the dominant partner of the survivors. But first Italy had to be wrested from Maxentius. Rome was the prize and Constantine knew that the Augustus who ruled from there might become the true ruler of the Empire. So in 312 he mobilised his troops. Legions had to be left to guard the frontiers, so his expeditionary force was far smaller than the armies of Maxentius. But he struck with irresistible skill, defeating the garrisons of Maxentius piecemeal in a series of swift battles, and by October he and his armies stood less than 20 miles from the gates of Rome.

While his outposts were fighting their delaying actions in northern Italy, Maxentius enrolled more troops, sent for re-inforcements from Africa and re-enlisted deserters from the armies of Severus and Galerius. With these abundant forces he was able to order a large army out of the city to destroy the legions of Constantine.

His forces took up their position on the Tiber some 12 miles upstream from Rome, where the river was crossed by the Milvian Bridge. Alongside this he built a second bridge of boats, giving his troops a swift crossing and good lines of communication. Their rear thus secured, they confidently awaited the assault of Constantine. On 28 October, the anniversary of his taking power and therefore an auspicious day, Maxentius marched out of the city to join his hitherto unconquered legions, certain that nightfall would see his rival destroyed, and he himself master of all the western provinces.

But a dramatic event had taken place in Constantine's camp on the eve of the battle, to understand which we must glance at the way Christianity was advancing throughout the Empire. Despite the savage persecutions, the faith was now well established in most of the major cities. Its doctrines had become the topic for sophisticated argument among the philosophers of Greece, the politicians of Asia Minor, the citizens of North Africa and the intelligentsia of Rome. They were not unknown in the ranks of the army. Indeed one of the reasons recorded for Diocletian's persecutions was the obduracy of a Christian soldier in refusing to wear on parade a decoration that he had won in battle. Constantine had seen much of the progress of Christianity. In York, where he had been acclaimed Caesar, there was almost certainly a Christian community. He had been in Nicomedia (guest and hostage of Diocletian) when the edict for the persecution was published. He had been present when Diocletian's palace had been destroyed by fire shortly afterwards; many had seen in the incident the hand of an avenging god and this possibility had made a deep impression on his mind.

Rome had always known that it could prosper only with the blessings of the gods. Constantine had seen the Empire torn by civil wars—wars due to the worship of power by ambitious commanders, heedless of the ancient deities. Was it as a result of this neglect of the divine that ruin now threatened the Roman world? Constantine had seen the constant devotion of the Christians to their God. Perhaps it was their total devotion to a divine force that had made them invulnerable to the attacks of the state. So perhaps theirs was the worship most pleasing to the divine influences, and it was their God who should become the guardian of Rome's stability, the giver of prosperity and the bestower of victory.

On the day before the battle Constantine's situation was precarious; far from his base, encamped within a countryside controlled by Maxentius, he knew that the morning would decide his destiny. Now, when victory flew hesitantly over the sleeping armies, uncertain upon which leader to place her laurels, perhaps the issue might be decided by the divine forces, and he who followed the true worship would triumph.

Constantine later claimed that he had that night seen in the sky a bright vision depicting the Christian faith. Some accounts say that it was the Cross and some the Chi-rho, the Greek monogram of Christ's name. Round the emblem he saw the words *In hoc signe vince* 'In this sign conquer'. Having been thus directly instructed of the divine will, Constantine immediately ordered the sacred emblem to be painted on his men's shields and during the night his artificers made a jewelled standard embodying not the eagle but the sign of Christ. And when in the morning his legions moved to attack, the Christian emblem for the first time led the battle line. The troops of Maxentius were routed, he himself dying in the fighting, and Constantine entered the city in triumph. Six short years ago he had sailed from Britain in his pursuit of power. Now he could sit in the house of the Caesars, master of the West, and the greatest figure in the Empire.

All Rome welcomed him on his *adventus* or formal entry into the City. The Senate voted him a triumphal arch, which stands to this day. He was cheered by the citizens and honours were showered upon him. Yet there was one strange omission from the ceremonies he performed. Unlike his predecessors he did not visit the temple of Jove on the Capitoline Hill, Rome's most sacred shrine. Having seen in the battle the efficacy of the new faith, he was not risking divine wrath by the worship of any deity other than the Christian God.

In the following year (313) Licinius and he met at Milan
to confirm their alliance. Constantine dominated the conference: first he arranged for Licinius to marry his half-sister
Constantia; and then he insisted upon the publication of an
edict, signed both by Licinius and himself, legalising Christianity and restoring all confiscated property to the churches
throughout the Empire. The Edict of Milan marked the foundation of the church as a political institution and the final identi-
fication of Constantine—as yet unbaptised—with the Christian
faith.

If Constantine was to fulfil his aim of re-establishing the
tetrarchy, then Maximinus had to be vanquished. In his own
eastern lands Maximinus continued to harass the Christians,
seeking to re-establish the worship of the old gods. Partly
moved by ambition and partly in a desperate bid to strike
down his rivals before they destroyed him, Maximinus invaded
the territory of Licinius, and in April 313 their legions met
in battle. The armies of Maximinus were scattered and he
himself barely escaped with his life by disguising himself as
a slave. He made his way as a fugitive to Tarsus, deep in the
safety of his own dominions, but there he fell sick and died,
leaving Constantine in the West and Licinius in the East as
the two Augusti. For ten years the two men were uneasily
content to share the mastery of the world.

Constantine had to defend the Rhine and Danube frontiers
against the barbarians, and won the glory to be gained in
defeating them; he possessed the city of Rome, the most
ancient jewel in the regalia of the state. But Rome was
rapidly diminishing in importance. Still the repository of
tradition, she was no longer the source of power. The main-
stream of events was flowing north of the Alps and Rome lay
in quiet water. Constantine ruled the western Empire from
Gaul, whence he could more easily protect it. On the other
hand, Licinius's realm comprised the wealth of the East, the
trade routes between Europe and Asia, many peaceful and
prosperous cities, and the growth and vigour of a new
culture.

For a year the two men eyed one another with envy and

suspicion. Then in 314 Licinius, without consulting Constantine, bestowed the title of Caesar Augustus upon one of his commanders, Aurelius Valerius Valens. Coins of the new Emperor were issued from the mint of Alexandria, showing the pagan god Jupiter holding a winged victory, with the eagle of Rome at his feet. So much for the Edict of Milan, and so much for loyalty! Licinius saw Valens as a replacement for Constantine and open war was inevitable. After two indecisive battles the two men resumed their uneasy peace, but Constantine was able to insist upon the deposition and execution of Valens, who paid with his life for the brief glory he enjoyed as Caesar Augustus.

Within a year Licinius had lost Greece, Macedonia and all the lower valley of the Danube. Two years later there was an attempt at reconciliation and the two Augusti by mutual agreement appointed three Caesars. In these arrangements Constantine emerged as the dominant figure, for of the three Caesars two were his sons, Crispus and the younger Constantine. Licinius appointed only one, his son, also named Licinius.

War between the two broke out afresh in 323. Licinius, repeating the disastrous example of Valens, renewed his challenge to Constantine's authority by appointing another of his commanders, Martinian, as Caesar Augustus. Constantine swiftly took up the challenge. His armies marched and in September 324 defeated those of Licinius, who, with his son, was allowed to live in retirement. But Licinius obstinately continued to strive against Constantine and once more contrived to make war. His armies were again crushingly defeated and now Constantine's mercy was exhausted. Licinius and his puppet co-emperor Martinian were both put to death and Constantine became the sole master of the Roman world.

All pretence that the Empire was republican in form had now been swept aside. Constantine lived unashamedly as a monarch, a remote and majestic figure, approachable only through his chamberlain and other officers of his sacred household. To meet him was a privilege granted to few, and to kiss the hem of his purple garment was an ineffable honour. The

Praetorian Guard had been disbanded and, though the office of Prefect remained, its holder was now a political minister. In place of the Senate, Constantine consulted a consistory of advisers. Society was hierarchical, with men ranking as Most Illustrious, Most Excellent and Most Honourable. Constantine himself was His Clemency; his household was divine and his decisions sacred.

He raised another of his sons, Constantius, to the rank of Caesar, and now the whole of the empire was under his sway. He planned the Empire's administration on the basis of political and geographical realities. Rome was no longer of strategic importance. Constantine believed that the eastern province held the future of the Empire. Accordingly he decided to rebuild the old city of Byzantium as a new Rome, on the crossroads between Europe and Asia. He named it "Constantine's City"—Constantinople. It was defended by mighty walls within which he built stately buildings for the worship of the God of the Christians and of the Divine wisdom. The arts of the mosaic worker, jeweller, painter and sculptor were lavished on the gleaming city, and libraries were filled with the learning of Greece and Rome. When Rome itself fell to the barbarians less than a century later, the arts and sciences of the classical world were preserved in the stout fortress of Constantinople. From this stronghold, centuries later, there came flooding back all the light of Rome, to re-illumine the barbarous kingdoms of Europe. It was the source of the Renaissance, the rebirth of knowledge of the civilisations of Greece and Rome, the scattering of the darkness and the dawn of modern Europe.

During this period Constantine suffered a personal tragedy. His wife Fausta, seeing Crispus (son of his first wife Minervina) as a rival to her own sons, accused the young man of treasonable intercourse with herself. This was adultery, incest, and blasphemy against the divine household. Constantine had Crispus put to death. Later when he learned the truth of Fausta's treachery, he had her executed in the public baths of Trèves. To replace Crispus he appointed his youngest son Constans to the rank of Caesar, giving the same title to two of his nephews, Haniballinus and Delmatius. The Empire was thus divided between his three sons (Constantine, Constantius and Constans) and two nephews, and he governed the civilised world through these obedient kinsmen.

Constantine busied himself with Church matters, resolving many of the theological arguments that were in danger of splitting the Christian community. A universal Creed was drawn up by a conference at Nicaea over which he presided. His mother Helena visited the Holy Land, and built a great church, gleaming with marble and mosaics, over Christ's birthplace. She brought back the True Cross, which she claimed to have discovered in Jerusalem. Constantine and his family never forgot the debt they owed to the Christian God for the victory at the Milvian Bridge, and for the subsequent prosperity of their Empire.

In 337 Constantine died at Nicomedia after a brief illness. He had been baptised a few days before and met his death not in the purple robes of an emperor but in the white vestments of a catechumen. His body was embalmed, sealed in a coffin of solid gold and taken for burial to his own city of Constantinople.

With the massive authority of Constantine dissolved in death, the unity which he had established did not long endure. The empire was parcelled out between his sons. The eldest, Constantine II, took the Atlantic provinces of Gaul, Spain and Britain; Constantius II received Asia, Thrace and the north African provinces westwards as far as Cyrenaica; Constans, the youngest, took the remaining African provinces, Italy, Greece and the lands bordering the Adriatic.

That Constantine had left three able sons was seen by many as a good augury for the future. But lust for power was stronger than the ties of blood and it was not long before the three Augusti were at one another's throats. First, Constantius in the East slaughtered all the descendants of his grandfather Constantius Chlorus save two of his cousins, Gallus and Julian. Three years later in 340 Constantine II invaded Italy to oust his brother Constans, but was ambushed near Aquileia and, after a brief struggle, cut down. His armies, recognising where power lay, went over to Constans, who now became Augustus of the western world.

In 343 Constans visited Britain, where, like his grandfather before him, he waged a victorious campaign against the Picts and the Scots. On the Continent he ruled effectively, recognising that his main task in the West was the defence of the Rhine and Danube frontiers against the menace of the barbarians. But the harsh lessons of the previous century had been forgotten. A man named Magnentius, a Gaul by birth from the region of Amiens, and one of the Empire's outstanding generals, had served with distinction in the armies of Constans. Early in 350 he secured the support of the legions and proclaimed himself Emperor in Gaul. Constans, with a surprising lack of resolution, retreated westwards towards Spain. A detachment of Magnentius's troops set out in pursuit, overtook him in the foothills of the Pyrenees and there slew him. The blood of two of Constantine's sons had now been spilled. Magnentius, his authority based on military skill and the support of the army, ruled over the western provinces, which Constantius II, Emperor in the East, decided to recover. He prepared a large army to attack Magnentius, while the latter prepared to defend himself.

During this time of uncertainty, two other men briefly enjoyed the title of Caesar Augustus. In Rome a nephew of Constantine named Nepotian proclaimed himself emperor. For twenty-eight days he wore the purple and there was just time for the mint to issue coins bearing his portrait and the title of Augustus; then he was captured and slain by soldiers loyal to Magnentius.

Meanwhile in Illyria the legions hesitated, undecided whether to support Constantius II or Magnentius. Constantine's sister, widow of Licinius, was living in Illyria, still a figure of great authority. Perhaps in the hope of obtaining independent power, she persuaded the Illyrian legions to proclaim their commander Vetranio as Augustus. He marked his loyalty to the house of Constantine by striking coins with the legend *hoc signo victor eris*—a variation of the divine injunction given to Constantine.

Magnentius consolidated his hold upon the western provinces and, as if to found a dynasty, bestowed the title of Caesar upon his younger brother Decentius. Then, Constantius II, his military preparation made, led his armies out of the East to destroy his rival. At first the generalship of Magnentius prevailed, but in September 351 he suffered a massive defeat at Mursa and retreated into Gaul, which he continued to govern for a further two years. But Constantius II did not relax his efforts, and finally vanquished him at Mount Seleucus in August 353. With his dream of empire shattered, Magnentius was deserted by his soldiers, and in despair he took his own life. His brother Decentius followed his example. Among his supporters had been Martinus, Governor of Britain, and Constantius now sent Paulus, a civil servant, to arrest him. Martinus resisted, sword in hand, and finally killed himself.

Constantius II was now the only Augustus and the Empire was again reunited. Like his father, Constantius II continued as sole Emperor, appointing two of his relatives as Caesars. First was Constantius Gallus, his cousin, who was put in charge of the eastern province, which he governed from the city of Antioch. But his rule was harsh and there were complaints. Constantius II summoned him to Milan to answer the charges; but before he arrived, he was arrested, tried, condemned to death and executed at Pola in the winter of 354.

Gallus had a half-brother named Julian, a nephew of Constantine the Great and cousin to Constantius II, who had always lived apart from the court with no expectation of power. More scholar than soldier, he had spent his life studying the literature and philosophy of Greeks, and unlike his imperial kinsmen, he had little sympathy for the Christians. He looked rather to Zeus, father of gods and men, and to the ancient divinities of Olympus. His cousin Constantius II treated him not merely with neglect but with hostility. Some of the odium earned by his half-brother Gallus had fallen upon him, and when Gallus was executed Julian was imprisoned for a while; afterwards he returned to Greece to follow the studies which so entranced him. It must, therefore, have been to his great surprise when, in 355 he was sent for by Constantius

and ceremonially invested with the title of Caesar. Within a
few days he was married to Constantius's sister, Helena, and
almost immediately he left to take up his command in Gaul.
The province was sorely beset. A little while before, a Frankish
leader named Silvanus had usurped the title of Augustus in
Cologne. He had been immediately overcome but now Cologne
had been sacked by a force of barbarians from beyond the
Rhine. Julian, whom many had dismissed as a bookish
dilettante, proved outstanding as a commander and quickly
gained the veneration of his troops. Men likened him to the
warlike Titus and the victorious Trajan, at the same time com-
paring him with Antoninus Pius for virtue and Marcus
Aurelius for learning.

When news came from Britain of further invasions by the
Picts and Scots, Julian took the threat seriously and sent to the
island Lupicinus, his *Magister Militum*, or Master of the
Armies. The campaign was inconclusive as Lupicinus had to
rush back to Gaul because of important developments there.

In 359 the Persians had renewed their attacks and Constantius, leaving the defence of the Danube to his subordinates,
led an army to oppose them. He then sent despatches to Julian
requesting reinforcements. The legions of Gaul were reluctant
to undertake a campaign so far from their base, and Julian
himself suspected that Constantius's demand was really based
upon a desire to limit his own military strength; he felt that
his successes in Gaul, and the affection in which he was held
by his legions, had made him a target for Constantius's
jealousy.

Rather than march the weary way to Asia, the soldiers in
Paris swore they would stay with him, and enthusiastically
acclaimed him as Augustus. He accepted their acclamation and
assumed the authority of Emperor. Constantius II, preoccupied
with his Persian campaign, took no steps to check Julian. He
had fought a number of indecisive battles against the Persian
king, had engaged in complex diplomatic negotiations, and
was striving to establish a firm and final frontier.

But Julian realised that he would ultimately have to make
good his new title by force of arms. His troops, who had been

L

unwilling to march the long roads eastwards in support of
Constantius, gladly followed him along the same roads to
confront the legions of the Orient. Constantius II assembled an
army and turned north to make war upon his defiant cousin.
By the winter of 361 he had marched as far as Cilicia, but
there he contracted a fever and there, in November, he died.
The three sons of Constantine the Great, once the hope of
the empire, were now all dead—Constantine II slaughtered
in the ambush at Aquileia, Constans butchered in the foothills
of the Pyrenees and Constantius, his power challenged, dying
of a sudden sickness.

Julian, now master of the Roman world and sole Augustus,
proved himself a worthy successor to his uncle, Constantine.
The latter's sons had been overshadowed by their father,
whose style and policies they felt compelled to follow. Like
him they issued coins with Christian emblems; like him they
wore the diadem; like him they discarded the beard and
cropped hair of the fighting Illyrian Emperors, and showed to
their people clean-shaven and delicate profiles. Julian discarded all these symbols except the diadem. The slogans upon
his coins were concerned not with Christ but with the glory
of the republic, the manhood of his armies and the safety of
the state. He wore the full beard of the philosopher, and was
as much at home in the gown of a scholar as in the breastplate of a soldier. He reversed the policy of Constantine, under
whom the Christian God had become the dominant deity, with
ambitious bishops having more influence with the Emperor
than magistrates or commanders; but he did not actively
persecute the Christian faith. Instead, he allowed total religious
toleration, giving all religions equality before the law. He was
not philosophically opposed to monotheism, and was extremely generous to the Jews, whose Temple in Jerusalem he
lavishly restored to its former splendour.

Once imperial support was withdrawn from the Christians,
it became evident that the unity which bound them had been
imposed and maintained largely by the power of Constantine
and his successors. Julian's edict of toleration suddenly
revealed the concealed dissensions within the Church: there

was fighting between sect and sect, old scores were paid off, bishops were lynched by their Christian opponents, and ugly violence spread through the streets of the great cities. Julian laid some mild disabilities upon the Christians—they were allowed neither to teach nor to proselytise—but there were no executions and no torture. He was content to watch their violent quarrels and angry disunity with tolerant amusement.

Meanwhile the ancient cults were revived throughout the Empire. In Cirencester a carved stone altar was dedicated to the old gods by the local governor. History has unfairly stigmatised Julian as 'The Apostate', suggesting that he had lapsed from the Christian faith. His admirers who called him Julian the Philosopher may have been nearer the truth. Throughout his life he had venerated the ancient deities, though, as a loyal subject of Constantine (and still more as his kinsman), he had to conform outwardly with the new religion. He was a man of many talents: a great soldier like the Illyrian emperors, a brilliant administrator like Augustus, and a philosopher like Marcus Aurelius. He was a prolific writer both of books and of letters to his friends. As a fighting commander, he was brave enough to hazard his own life on the field of battle; and his dash in attack and resolution when assailed won him the unstinted acclaim of his legions.

In 363, after he had been Emperor for two years, the Persians renewed their attacks. Julian once more buckled on his armour and led the legions of the East against them. With him as second-in-command went Jovianus, captain of his household troops. In the summer, in a fierce encounter with the Persian forces, Julian died on the battlefield, sword in hand. With their gallant Emperor dead and with the Persians still undefeated, the officers had to take a swift decision. A successor had to be found on the spot, to take command. Their choice fell upon Jovian, who immediately assumed office. To Procopius, a kinsman of the dead Julian and a fighting commander of considerable reputation, was entrusted the task of bearing the corpse of Julian to Tarsus where it was buried with all solemnity.

The legions had been badly mauled by the Persians and

Jovian's first thought was for the safety of his army. He dropped the aggressive plans of the dead Julian and in July 363, made peace with the Persians who imposed harsh terms. Jovian had to surrender almost all the frontier territories won by Diocletian. The Empire, ashamed, considered the settlement dishonourable, and Jovian secured peace at the cost of his own reputation. During the winter he marched through the surrendered territories towards Constantinople, but ill luck still dogged him. He broke his journey at Dadastana in Galatia. It was now February and the nights were cold, and his servants brought a brazier containing a charcoal fire into his bedroom. Jovian went gratefully to his warm bed, but the room was ill-ventilated and in the morning they found him dead, suffocated by the fumes.

Jovian was a Christian and during his brief reign the Church regained her former dominance. The work of Julian was undone and the old gods were finally banished from the Roman world.

Valentinianus was a high-ranking general, forty-three years old, who had served with distinction under both Julian and Jovian, and on Jovian's death, after lengthy consultations, he was chosen as Augustus. He decided to return to the old concept of two emperors, and at once bestowed the rank of Augustus upon his younger brother Valens. Valentinian ruled the West and Valens the East. Each of the brothers on their gold coins proclaimed himself *Restitutor Rei Publicae*—the Restorer of the Republic. In spite of the monarchical principle imposed by Constantine, there were still men who looked back with admiration to the first days of the Principate. Perhaps Julian's attitudes had revived a general interest in the past, reminding men of the origins of Rome's greatness. Certainly the reign of Valentinian and Valens, lasting eleven years and more, provided an interval of sunshine between the dark storm clouds that were rolling over Europe.

Valentinian stemmed the barbarian tide in the West largely through his wise choice of generals. Events in Britain provided an example both of his difficulties and his methods. In 368 he was campaigning in north-eastern Gaul when news came from

Britain that the Picts and Scots were again raiding the province. They had been joined by the Saxons from beyond the Rhine, who had sailed to the island in search of easy booty. With them, too, were the Attacotti, probably from Ireland. The four nations were working in concert as the result of some formal barbarian alliance. This was typical of what was happening on all the frontiers. The nations outside the Empire had for generations seen the rich Roman provinces—as traders, as immigrants or as enlisted men. They had been dazzled by the wealth and sparkle of the civilised lands, seeing them as fine places for loot and pillage. With the awesome name of Constantine and his descendants blown as dust upon the winds of time, they knew that their hour had come.

Valentinian summoned from his army his most famous general, Count Theodosius. (The title of *Comes*, Companion of the Emperor, had ceased to mean merely a councillor. It was now borne by generals leading mobile forces to points of danger, representing the person of the Emperor and the power of Rome. From the word *Comes* medieval Europe derived the title Count.) As many troops as could be spared were detached from Valentianian's army in Gaul, and with them Count Theodosius crossed the Channel. In Britain he found the defences in total disarray. The barbarians were ranging the countryside at will, pillaging the cities and enslaving the inhabitants. London itself was under siege. Theodosius drove back the besiegers, made London his base, prepared his armies during the winter, and by the spring of 369 moved to the attack. In a swift campaign he cleared the country as far north as Hadrian's Wall. Many of the Wall's buildings had been destroyed and many of its defences thrown down. Theodosius organised fatigue parties to repair the damage and the marks of his soldiers' handiwork are still to be seen. The Count had internal as well as external military problems in the island: he had to quell a rebellion and execute the ringleader; and had to disband one local military unit of doubtful loyalty.

To mark the overwhelming success of the Roman armies Valentinian gave the name of Valentia to one of the provinces of Britain. London, as a mark of imperial esteem, was renamed *Augusta*; but the old name was already venerable and, after a while the city reverted to, and still retains, its ancient name.

Valentinian had two sons—Gratianus, who was born in 360 by his first wife, Severa; and Valentinian born in 371 by his second wife, Justina. In 367, when Gratian was only seven years old, he was given the rank of Augustus, nominally to rule equally with his father.

In the East Valentinian's brother Valens was working with equal resolution. The barbarians along the Danube were renewing their attacks on the dying Empire. To the south the Persian threat, against which Rome had now laboured for three centuries, was vigorously renewed. In 365 Valens set out for Syria to meet that threat. Back at Constantinople Procopius, who had borne Julian's body back to Tarsus for burial, seized the opportunity of Valens' absence to exploit his kinship with Julian and with the now legendary house of Constantine, to assume the title of Augustus. He projected himself as the restorer of the great days of the Constantinian dynasty, his coins bearing the slogan *Reperatio Felicia Temporis*, which can be roughly translated as 'happy times are here again'! But his glory was short-lived. Valens, in spite of his preoccupations in Syria, moved swiftly against him, scattering his armies and killing Procopius himself in the summer of 366.

In 375 Valentinian was at his headquarters in Pannonia, engaged on the unending task of checking the invaders. At a meeting with a barbarian deputation, he was so angered by their insolence that he suffered a stroke and died shortly afterwards. Now, when the Empire was crumbling, men were desperate to retain dynastic continuity. Accordingly Valentinian's son, Valentinian II, though only four years old, was proclaimed Augustus of the West a few days after his father's death. His elder brother, Gratian already held that rank. For two years, with boys on the throne of the West, Valens upheld the whole of the Empire.

A year after Valentinian's death the Visigoths, whose homelands were being invaded by the Huns, sought refuge on the Roman side of the Danube. Valens allowed them to come as settlers, but the local inhabitants took unkindly to their new neighbours. Resentment flared into open war. The Visigoths tore up their treaty, stood to arms and rode out to pillage Moesia and Thrace; and Valens had once more to take the field against them. At Hadrianopolis occurred one of the most decisive battles of the ancient world. The Visigoths, for the most part mounted, confronted the steadfast legions, who for generations had been masters of the world's battlefields. Now they were faced by cavalry using the newly invented stirrup, a discovery that revolutionised the art of war. The Gothic cavalrymen could fight securely from the saddle, outmanoeuvring the opposing infantry. The Roman army was cut to pieces and, when the fighting was over, Valens lay dead upon the trampled and bloodstained field.

The remaining Augusti were now the eleven-year-old Gratian and the seven-year-old Valentinian II. Tragically the great Count Theodosius had been put to death by Valens, and his son, who had inherited his father's military genius, had withdrawn from public affairs and was living quietly in retirement. After the disaster of Hadrianopolis it was decided that the prowess of Theodosius, the dead count's son, should be enlisted to support the two boy Emperors. So Theodosius was declared Augustus in January 379. His most urgent task was to restore the lost provinces in the East and to re-establish the reputation of Roman arms. For two years he fought steadfastly against the barbarians and, behind the shield of his armies, the eastern Empire made a brief recovery.

Dramatic events in Britain suddenly called him westwards. As a young man he had served in the island, where he had known a Spanish officer, Magnus Maximus. Theodosius now sat in Constantinople, clad in the majesty of his semi-divine office, while Magnus Maximus was still a regimental officer serving in Britain. The latter had before him the golden example of Constantine, who, using Britain as his base and its legions as the nucleus of an army, had achieved world power. So in 383 he assembled all the best soldiers in Britain, stripping Hadrian's Wall of its garrisons and the military bases of their troops, and led them across the Channel into Gaul, where he set up his standard as Magnus Maximus Augustus, Emperor of the West.

For a while he was successful. On the Rhine he routed the barbarians and re-established Rome's ancient frontier. He then swung southwards, across Gaul, and entered Spain. His armies, encouraged by victory and thirsty for further glory, now occupied all the Atlantic provinces, while Gratian's dominions had dwindled to the peninsula of Italy. Gratian sought safety in Rome, among the fading traditions of the past, but on his journey was overtaken and slain. Maximus, by force of arms, was now Augustus of the West. For a year or two he allowed young Valentinian II to rule over Italy. But in 388 he assembled an army to march on Rome.

In the East Theodosius watched Maximus grow in greatness, content that the Empire was well served by the usurper's victories over the barbarians; but learning of Maximus's intention to invade Italy, he mobilised the legions of the East, and with these overwhelming forces marched to the defence of Valentinian II. So the two men who had once served together in the army of Britain confronted one another near Aquileia as enemies. The legions of the East triumphed and Maximus was captured. In Theodosius's heart there was no room for memories of former friendship, and Maximus was executed by the troops of his former companion in the summer of 388. As part of his preparations for the invasion of Italy, Maximus had declared his son Flavius Victor head of the western Empire. After Aquileia, Flavius Victor was also put to death.

With Maximus destroyed, Theodosius entered Rome in triumph and spent two years in Italy. He re-established Valentinian as Augustus of the West but the boy proved an ineffectual ruler. It was his generals who held true power, and he was murdered by one of these, named Arbogastes, in 392. Arbogastes did not seize power but set up a puppet emperor in the person of Eugenius, a senior imperial official. Eugenius was not a soldier and had been professor of rhetoric and grammar before entering the imperial service. For two years Arbogastes ruled in the West, content to leave nominal political supremacy in the weak hands of the academic Eugenius.

Theodosius, now some fifty years old, had two sons— Arcadius, born in 377, and Honorius, born in 384. In 383 Theodosius had raised Arcadius (still only five years old) to the rank of Augustus, and he did the same for Honorius in 393.

In 394 Theodosius led his armies into Italy to overthrow Eugenius and Arbogastes. Age had not diminished his military genius. In northern Italy he broke the legions of Arbogastes, and captured Eugenius and put him to death. Arbogastes escaped the carnage of the battle but later took his own life.

Two barbarian nations in particular were now menacing the Empire—the Goths and the Vandals. The Goths were a Germanic people who had lived on the Baltic shores. In the second century they migrated southwards, and by the third century had settled between the Danube and the Black Sea. There they soon came into conflict with the Roman frontier forces, and in 251 inflicted a crushing defeat upon the Roman army in Moesia. For nearly 20 years after that they controlled much of the eastern Empire. They destroyed the temple of Diana at Ephesus, pillaged Athens and ravaged Greece.

After Claudius the Illyrian had smashed their armies in 269, winning the title of *Gothicus*, Aurelian had permitted them to settle along the left bank of the Danube and for a century there was peace. Under Constantine most became Christians. (There exist to this day fragments of a Gothic translation of the Bible, made by their Bishop, Ulfilas.) By the middle of the fourth century Ermanric, their king, held sway from the Gulf of Bothnia to the Black Sea; he was famous in Germanic folk-lore and is mentioned in early Anglo-Saxon poetry.

The Vandals were kin and subject to the Goths. Constantine had settled many of them in Pannonia as Treaty Troops, whose descendants became Christians. Their nobles wore the uniform of Roman officers, learned much of the arts of war, and were not blind to the weaknesses of Roman society.

Two senior officers from these nations served under Theodosius. One was Stilicho, a Vandal. By 384, he was *Magister Equitum*, commander-in-chief of the cavalry, and carried out important negotiations with the Persians. He was promoted to the command of all the armies in the West and married Serena, a niece of Theodosius. In 394 he was appointed governor in Rome and was now one of the most powerful figures of the Empire. The second officer was Alaric, a Goth; he was commander of a Gothic detachment and had fought in Theodosius's campaign against Eugenius. These two men were to be pitted against one another, the one as the last effective champion of the western Empire, and the other as the instrument of that Empire's final overthrow.

Five months after defeating Eugenius and Arbogastes, Theodosius fell ill at Milan and died, swollen with dropsy, in January 395. Thenceforward events moved mercilessly towards the end of Rome's greatness. Arcadius, now eighteen, reigned at Constantinople, wearing the diadem and dressed in purple, but leaving the government to others. The Praetorian Prefect for many years was a man named Rufinus, and he was the effective ruler of the East.

In 395 Alaric the Goth was tempted by the weakness of the eastern Government to throw off his allegiance. He invaded Thrace, Macedonia and Thessaly. Finally, by seizing Illyria, he became master of all the lands between the Adriatic and Aegean seas. He besieged Athens, compelling its citizens to pay a huge ransom for the preservation of their ancient city. He crossed into the Peleponnese, plundering and laying waste the countryside.

Stilicho, now Master of the Armies of the West, marched his legions to the rescue. Alaric retreated safely into Illyria, carrying off numerous captives and immense plunder. The ministers of Arcadius, impotent against the warlike Alaric, appointed him Governor of Illyria. They hoped this high honour would purchase his loyalty and also demonstrate to the West that they remained independent and that the legions of Stilicho were less than welcome.

When Rufinus fell, Eutropius, a eunuch, took power into his own hands. Arcadius had been robed and perfumed, crowned and adored, since the age of five; small wonder that his will to govern was sapped and his independence destroyed. Remote from reality, he dwelt in the hushed and richly decorated rooms of the palace, heedless of the din of distant battle. He was married when he was eighteen to Eudoxia, daughter of a Frankish officer. She bore him a son, named Theodosius after his grandfather, who was declared Augustus in 402 when he was only nine months old. From then until her death in 404, Eudoxia, with the title of Augusta, became the effective ruler. After she died Arcadius still achieved no independence and the government fell into the hands of the new Praetorian Prefect, Anthemius.

In 408, aged 31, Arcadius died as he had lived, in isolation in the palace of Constantinople, and his seven-year-old son, Theodosius II, became the nominal ruler. With a child on the throne, Anthemius continued to be the true wielder of power.

Meantime the boy Honorius began a more prosperous reign as Augustus in the West. He was well served by Stilicho, who restored to Roman arms much of the glory of the past. One of his campaigns was fought in Britain. The armies there had been overwhelmed by a renewal of the barbarian alliance and both the Count and Duke of Britain slain. Stilicho, in a swift and terrible campaign, scattered and destroyed the invaders.

In 402 Alaric, now Governor of Illyria, marched his troops along the traditional invasion route round the Adriatic sea into northern Italy. Honorius hastily left Rome while the roads to the north lay open, and set up his court in the fortified city of Ravenna, behind whose walls he passively awaited the outcome of this challenge to his power. Once more it was Stilicho who rode to the rescue and Alaric, swinging north in pursuit of Honorius, found his path blocked by Stilicho's army. He attacked them at Pollentia but was forced to retreat, defeated, though not vanquished. For a year the two armies held their positions, both generals avoiding a direct confrontation.

In the following autumn, Stilicho advanced and utterly defeated Alaric near Verona. With superb generalship, Alaric regrouped his shattered forces and retreated in good order to Illyria. Thither went an embassy from Stilicho, with the authority of Honorius, seeking not war but an alliance. It was agreed that Alaric should switch his loyalties and march against Arcadius, supported by Stilicho's legions. But the expedition did not take place and Alaric demanded payment for the preparations he had made. The ministers of Honorius agreed to pay him the huge sum of 4,000lb of gold.

Meanwhile Stilicho returned to his tasks in the West. In 405 he smashed another barbarian host which had invaded Italy under its leader Radagaisus. Then, at the court in Ravenna, men began to murmur that he was growing covetous of the Emperor's power. Married to Theodosius's niece, father-in-law of Honorius (who had, in happier times, married his daughter), Master of the Armies, his eagles garlanded with many laurels, he would have been a worthy candidate for the rank of Augustus. Had fortune favoured him in the palace as she had on the battlefield, and had he in fact replaced Honorius, the history of the world might have been different. Rumours of his ambition, however, aroused the jealousy of the Emperor, and he was arrested and executed. So perished the last effective defender of the western Empire.

In 407 what was left of the legions in Britain saw in the chaos of Europe an opportunity to relive the days of Carausius, Maximus and Constantine, when the island had been the cradle of emperors. At Silchester in Hampshire (whose grey walls stand to this day), they raised a private soldier to the rank of Augustus for no better reason than that his name was Constantine, to such an extent had the golden example of the great emperor dazzled the armies of Britain! Under their new Augustus they crossed to the continent, where the new Constantine III made common cause with the barbarians. With their support he marched to Spain, which he added to his realms. But shortly afterwards Spain was overrun by the Vandals and other barbarians; his armies were defeated and his brief dream of glory ended. He was captured by the forces of Honorius and executed.

By the shores of the Adriatic Sea, in what was now virtually his independent kingdom of Illyria, Alaric had heard with grim satisfaction of the death of Stilicho. On the pretext that the promised gold had not been paid, he once more put his legions on a war footing. Confident that there was now no man sufficiently strong to oppose him, he invaded Italy, and, without meeting any effective resistance, advanced to the walls of Rome.

The Eternal City, once the proud mistress of the civilised world, now suffered the ignominy of a siege. Gone were the steadfast legions who had once defended her, and gone was the resolution of former days. Panic and rancour took the place of courage. Frustrated in their attempts to repel the besiegers, the citizens turned their anger against one another. Serena, Stilicho's widow, was executed on the grounds that she had been in communication with Alaric. First starvation and then death roamed the streets. Ravenna sent no help. When the Senate, parleying with Alaric, said that he would have to fight his way through the ranks of the citizens in arms, his reply was curt: 'The thicker the grass grows, the easier it is to scythe!' Finally, terms were agreed. Rome was to pay a ransom of 5,000lb of gold, 30,000lb of silver, together with bales of cloth, robes of silk and precious spices.

Alaric left Rome peacefully. But Ravenna answered his messages by sending against him 6,000 armed troops, which his army slaughtered almost to a man. At Ravenna there was neither wisdom nor policy. Contemptuous notes to Alaric that came ill from a powerless emperor, quarrels between the ministers, a total failure to face reality—all these showed how the last vestiges of authority had vanished from the pathetic figure of Honorius. Ministers bowed to him and kissed the hem of his robe, and generals discussed unreal strategy for non-existent armies. The painted rooms that should have been the centre of western power became a stage-setting for a meaningless tragi-comedy, acted out to the despair of whatever gods had once guided the destinies of Rome.

Alaric marched again to Rome, this time seizing the port of Ostia, through which the city received its corn supplies. Ships still came to the stout jetty built by Claudius, laden with the harvests of Egypt. Now Alaric's troops guarded the jetty and blocked the road to Rome; now indeed Alaric held the dagger of starvation to the throat of Senate and people. Still he did not seek the city's destruction. He was content to demand the appointment by the Senate of a new Augustus, and nominated Attalus, Prefect of the City, who was duly elected. One of the first acts of Attalus was to appoint Alaric Master of the Armies. The Gothic leader now stood at the height of his power.

Attalus, perhaps dazzled by his new titles of Augustus, the Dutiful, the Fortunate, was blind to the stark fact that he was emperor only by the sufferance of Alaric. He was of pure Roman descent and a member of an old aristocratic family. So it was contrary to the traditions of his house and his own inherited pride to accept for long that he was the nominee and creature of a mere barbarian. His bright diadem and purple robes awakened in his mind daydreams of power that extinguished the unwelcome reality. He remembered only that he was a Roman Emperor and soon forgot that he, like Rome itself, was now subject to the authority of Alaric.

The Senate, which had long been disatisfied that Honorius should have made his headquarters at Ravenna, leaving the City without any imperial presence, welcomed the appointment of Attalus. Misled by the Senate's enthusiasm and by his own hallucinations of power, he soon embarked upon independent and ambitious policies. First he sent a delegation to the African provinces and from them obtained recognition.

Then, accompanied by Alaric, upon whom his illusory power depended, he visited Ravenna to negotiate with officers of Honorius. At first the negotiations went well and the delegation from Ravenna agreed to recognise the appointment of Attalus and, following ancient precedent, it was agreed that the western empire should be divided between the two emperors—Honorius in Ravenna and Attalus in Rome. But this sensible settlement was rendered impossible by the insolence of Attalus. He insisted that Honorius should resign from his office and accept a life of exile. Since the world knew that behind the purple-clad figure of Attalus there stood the armoured ranks of Alaric's legions, the delegates of Honorius were intimidated and deserted their master. They acknowledged Attalus as the sole emperor, thus still further feeding his vanity. Honorius, in the depths of despair, received a fortunate reinforcement of 4,000 troops, who arrived unexpectedly at Ravenna and stoutly manned its defences, giving him a breathing space. Attalus now stood in peril of open war, for success in which he was solely dependent upon the army of Alaric. But all this he disregarded. Even when the province of Africa turned against him he forgot altogether the allegiance he owed to Alaric and continued to pursue his personal and impossible ambition.

Alaric, rightly incensed, publicly stripped him of the imperial diadem and the purple robes of his office, and kept him prisoner. Then, to show his contempt for his one-time nominee, he sent the imperial diadem and robes to Honorius as a mark of friendship and in recognition of Honorius's authority. So for a while he was content to live as Honorius's subordinate, but this did not long endure. Outraged by further insults heaped upon him by the powerless authorities of Ravenna, he marched against Rome for the third time.

This time there was no long siege. The slaves of Rome, remembering Alaric's kindness to them in the past, opened the gates. His armies entered the city on 24 August 410 and for six days the exultant soldiers looted and sacked the one-time capital of the world. Alaric ordered his men not to rob Christian churches nor—denying them the common reward of victorious troops—to rape the women. Within the limits of these orders there was a general and horrible massacre. Slaves joined the troops of Alaric, and butchered their masters. Parts of the city were burned and the treasures of centuries went to fill the knapsacks of the plundering soldiers.

After six days of horror the murder and pillage ceased. The troops reassembled, sated with blood and violence, and withdrew in a disciplined manner from the city. But those six days marked the end of the story. The Empire of the West was now dead and the labour of centuries was over. As the smoke cleared from the burning city, so was Rome's reputation of invincibility blown away on the morning wind. Now in Gaul, in Spain, in Britain and in all the lands along the Rhine and Danube, the eager barbarians set up their vigorous and triumphant kingdoms. Only in Constantinople, safe behind her stout walls, did the magical name of Augustus persist, far distant from the now humbled city where it was first spoken.

In Europe itself only the ghost of the Empire remained, and it was to be centuries before that ghost was exorcised. It walked in the retinue of Charlemagne, who saw himself as the successor of the Caesars. It haunted the palaces of the Holy Roman Empire and the distant court of the Czars. It strode beside Napoleon, who sought to rebuild in blood the shattered unity of Roman Europe, reviving the title of Consul, the eagle standards, the triumphal arch, and many other trappings of the vanished Empire of the Caesars.

Those same eagles, which took wing and fled from Rome on that dreadful August day in 410, still circle the globe. They became the badges of many of the new nations of Europe, who thus commemorated the ancient days of order and splendour. The Caesars, Romans and barbarians alike, the soldiers among them and the philosophers, the pagans and the Christians, had constructed and defended a system that civilised the lands of Europe, building cities and roads that survive to this day. They made possible the dissemination of the arts and learning of Greece, and of the compassion of Christianity, throughout all the lands between the Atlantic Ocean and the Euphrates, from the Yorkshire moors to the deserts of Africa. And though all seemed lost, their work endured. The Renaissance gave back to Europe the light that had vanished, and the purposes, methods and efficiency of Rome outlasted the broken marble of her buildings and justified the title she had borne so long—the Eternal City.

CONTINUITY

Constantinople -

From the Fifth Century onwards

In view of the savage destruction of Rome by Alaric, and the decay of the Empire (which was that destruction's first cause as well as its later consequence) how was it that so much of Rome survived? And how was it—her power shattered, her learning and techniques forgotten, her laws submerged in political chaos—that she nevertheless became (and largely remains) a major influence on the European scene?

True, the physical apparatus of the Empire remained in being. But much of this was used for the Empire's destruction. When we read of barbarian armies overrunning Italy or breaking into Spain, we must remember that it was along good Roman roads that they advanced, with milestones to mark their march, and towns to provide them with shelter at the end of each day's journey. Strong points and defence works still stood; but, once overwhelmed, they served those who had seized them. The military skills that Rome had bequeathed to the barbarians by recruiting them into her armies were used, as Alaric had used them, to sweep away the old order. Thus, with the new nations bent on military adventures and on the conquest of their neighbours, the legacy Rome had left in the west, of military works and martial skills, became in other hands the instruments of her overthrow.

It was not Western Europe but Constantinople, the New Rome into which Constantine had transformed the ancient city

M

of Byzantium, that preserved the treasures and skills of Rome, and gave them back to the West after many generations. Constantine, perhaps unknowingly, perhaps with the 'Divine Foresight' celebrated on so many coins, had built not merely a city but a bridge across the dark chasm of the centuries.

After the sack of Rome darkness began to fall over Western Europe. With the brave shield of the legions shattered, the barbarians were soon to smash their way across the frontiers and to occupy all the lands that Rome had once ruled, and upon which the light of Roman order and administration had once shone. Within half a century, for example, two German tribes from beyond the Rhine were to sail their ships across the North Sea, and to seize the island of Britain. There, advancing along the Roman roads, the Angles and Saxons gradually conquered the whole island. Within a few generations Rome's name became a faint folk memory. The great buildings, deserted and falling into ruins, were seen as the mysterious work of some forgotten race of giants. The Christian faith was extinguished by the warlike barbarians, except in the west and north of the island, where Roman learning for a while lingered.

The Franks, yet another German tribe, broke westwards into Gaul and there set up their kingdom, of which modern France is the successor. The Gaulish cities fell to the barbarians. In Paris, once the capital of the Celtic tribe of the Parisii, where Roman buildings and Roman baths still stood majestically, the Frankish kings established their royal seat and ruled the lands round about. The Burgundians, first the enemies and later the allies of Rome, set up their rival kingdom in the same province. Only in the far south of Gaul, in what had been one of the earliest of Rome's dominions, and which still retained the name of Provence (the Province), did Roman literature and Roman attitudes survive, in almost complete isolation from the rest of Europe. Poets and philosophers there continued the proud traditions of imperial days, and in the countryside of Provence the ghost of Rome walks to this day.

Spain too fell; native and barbarian kingdoms replaced the Roman order, established since republican days, and the patient

work of centuries was undone. The Goths and Visigoths overran Italy. The authority of warrior kings replaced the power of
Christian emperors. In almost all the lands of the Empire the
savage warhelm of fighting chieftains replaced the diadem and
radiate crown of the vanished Caesars.

But Constantinople stood firm. There the power of Rome
persisted, changed fundamentally by its transfer into eastern
lands, but retaining much of the old invincibility and resolution. There too learning survived. For when Constantine had
built and peopled his new city, he had filled its libraries with
Rome's own heritage of Greek and Latin literature. In the West
the illiterate barbarians and the literate but censorious Church,
in a strange alliance, almost totally destroyed all vestiges of
ancient learning. But the libraries and palaces of Constantinople
remained as safe repositories of ancient culture. Thus, though
Rome herself seemed to have forfeited her proud title of The
Eternal City, within the stout walls of Constantinople something survived of her institutions, her traditions and her learning. So, in the dark times, the wise conception of Diocletian
that there should be two centres of power in the Empire, and
the foresight of Constantine in transforming the ancient city
of Byzantium into a new Rome, were fully justified.

The Western Empire, despite the heroic efforts of Honorius's
general Constantius (who was himself declared Augustus in
417) rapidly decayed, and seventy years later the title of
Augustus had vanished. But in Constantinople for many
centuries Augustus after Augustus continued to reign.
Theodosius II, son of Arcadius, had been declared Augustus by
his father as a baby. Four years after the fall of Rome, when
Theodosius was a boy of thirteen, his sister Pulcheria became
the effective ruler of the Eastern Empire, which then comprised
all the provinces in Asia, together with Egypt, Thrace, Moesia,
Macedonia and Greece. When Theodosius died in 450,
Pulcheria appointed a sixty year old general, Marcian, to the
post of Augustus and took him as her husband. During the
reign of Leo, his successor, Constantinople was faced with the
possibility of disaster. Her armies by now consisted almost
entirely of mercenary foreigners, largely German, and there

was grave danger that the German military faction would overthrow the state and, as in the West, create their own kingdom.
But Leo, by recruiting loyal men from the provinces of his
eastern territories, outfaced the German party, ensured the
continued survival of his Empire, and so won for himself a
place in history. He was succeeded by his grandson Leo II, who
died after a brief reign of nine months.

Among the soldiers whom the elder Leo had recruited was
an Issaurian chieftain named Zeno, who had given good
service to the state and had married the emperor's daughter.
On the death of Leo II, Zeno was declared Augustus.

The sixth century opened with the reign of Anastasius, who
had been a minor official in the court of Zeno. After being
proclaimed Augustus, he married the daughter of the first Leo.
He reigned successfully for twenty-seven years, a careful administrator who consolidated the financial power of Constantinople.

He was succeeded by his nephew, the great Justinian, whose
reign lasted until 565. He is best remembered for having
gathered together all the laws of the empire into the famous
Justinian Code, from which many European nations were later
to derive their laws. He was a man of wide ambition who
dreamed of regaining the lost western provinces, thereby re-
creating the old empire. His legions recaptured Italy, Egypt and
Africa; they marched as far as Spain; and it seemed for a while
that all Europe might once more come under the rule of the
Augustus. He also fought long campaigns against the Persians,
the hereditary enemies of Rome, to secure the southern
frontiers. His armies were led by the great general Belisarius,
who received no greater reward for his services than a blind
and penurious old age. Poor Belisarius gained immortality not
for his military prowess, but by the legend that sees him as a
blind beggar standing in the streets, asking plaintively for 'A
copper, please, for Belisarius the general'.

Another feature of Justinian's reign was the hysterical
support of the population of Constantinople for the teams of
charioteers, the Blues and the Greens, who raced in the arena.
The supporters of the two teams rioted to the point of civil

war, and there was a time when Justinian was almost compelled to leave his capital. Violence among spectators of sport
is not a new phenomenon.

Justinian's dramatic military achievements were not carried
out without cost, and his successors in the sixth century,
Justinus, Tiberius and Maurice, faced not only military
problems but mounting economic difficulties. Moreover, new
enemies had appeared; for the Slavs were pressing on the
eastern frontiers. The century closed in tumult and mutiny.
Maurice was murdered by his army in 602 and the Eastern
Empire was now in disarray. But worse was to follow.

During the sixth century Mecca had seen the birth of
Mohammed, a man whose leadership of the Arabs was to have
cataclysmic consequences for Constantinople. The Eastern
Empire, true to the traditions of Constantine, was fundamentally Christian and the emperors were the leaders of a
Christian community. Holiness was their attribute as much as
majesty. For centuries, Christianity was the unchallenged faith
of Europe. The pagan religions of the barbarians had one by
one succumbed to the persuasion of Christian missionaries and
to the weight of Christian swords. Now Mohammed's new
teachings, calling his people back to the worship of the one
true God, were to unify the Arabs and to make them a warlike
and aggressive people. Christianity, for the first time for
centuries, was to be faced by a rival faith and was to be put to
the dreadful test of war.

During the early part of the seventh century, Constantinople
acquired an emperor of a stature to match the difficulties of
the times. Heraclius, son of the Governor of Africa, was
declared Augustus in 610 and proved to be one of the most
heroic figures the Eastern Empire ever produced. He strove for
twelve years to stabilise its finances and to rebuild its shattered
armies. But for all his efforts, he met with little success. Egypt
was lost in 616 and in 622 the northern boundaries of his
Empire were threatened. Then the Persians captured Jerusalem.
Until its conquest by the Persians, Christians could visit the
Holy Places freely and in safety, and the occupation of the
Holy City by a heathen power was seen as an intolerable

affront to Christendom. Jerusalem must be freed. To support the war the wealthy churches of Constantinople made gifts of coin and treasure. An army was organised and, in six brilliant campaigns, Heraclius defeated the Persians and made a victorious peace in 622.

Ominously, it was at that very time that Mohammed, now at the height of his power, had addressed a letter to all the kings and potentates of the known world, inviting them to join in the worship of Allah and to join the ranks of Islam. His followers, the Saracens, were on the march. They overran Syria, and by the middle of the century only Alexandria remained of Constantinople's Egyptian possessions.

Heraclius died in 641 and it seemed that the brief glory of his reign was to be merely a prelude to further disaster. The citizens of Constantinople, forgetful of the military power that had been their safeguard for centuries, became preoccupied with sterile theological arguments. In a divided city it began to appear that the days of the Eastern Empire were numbered, and that the Christian city of Constantine was to be submerged in the rising tide of Islam.

In 673 the Saracens crossed into Europe and besieged Constantinople for four weary years. Her strong walls and the renewed resolution of her citizens repulsed all attacks and the city did not fall. But all her lands in Asia fell to the Saracens and most of her lands in Europe were seized by the Bulgarians. The Eastern Empire now comprised little more than the city of Constantinople itself.

Early in the eighth century another Leo, a general in the east, became Augustus. Under his martial leadership a second siege of the Saracens was repulsed. His armies moved to the attack and by the time of his death in 741 Asia Minor had been regained for Christendom.

But later in the same century, Crete and Sicily were lost to the Saracens. Constantinople now failed to seize new opportunities to revive her Empire's lost greatness. The Bulgarians had been converted to Christianity and were no longer a threat. The Mohammedan world was torn by strife and the once-unified empire of the Caliphs was breaking up. Emperors and people alike disregarded these opportunities and again theological arguments divided the city and distracted men's minds from temporal problems. The churches had for centuries been decorated with mosaics, paintings and statues of God the Father, of Christ and of the saints. There now arose a party of austerity which demanded the total destruction of these images or icons. The struggle between these, the iconoclasts, and those who wished to retain the physical depictions of the divine, occupied men's minds for many years. Violence and disorder ensued and the real enemies were forgotten.

There now took place a series of distant events that were to have great consequences for the Eastern Empire. Charles, King of the Franks, had for thirty-two years led his armies in the defence of Christianity and the enlargement of his own dominions. He had marched into Italy to defend Pope Adrian I against the Lombards, whom he conquered. He fought the Saracens in Spain and ruled that land as far as the Ebro. He fought victoriously against the Bavarians, the Saxons and many other nations. Once more the western world had a Christian champion, who saw himself as the defender not merely of his own Frankish kingdom, but of many of the lands of the vanished Empire. Finally, on Christmas Day 800, he was crowned in Rome as Augustus, Roman Emperor of the West. He took the name of *Carolus Magnus*, Charles the Great. His own people called him Charlemagne and it is by this name that he is remembered, a worthy successor to the vanished Caesars whose title he had assumed and whose glories he sought to revive.

The immediate effect of all this was to divide Christianity in two. There were now two emperors, one in the East and one in the West, each a Christian leader, and the Augustus in Constantinople at last had a rival. Thenceforward there were to be two distinct branches of Christianity—the 'Latins' in the nations of western Europe, and the 'Romans' in the lands ruled by Constantinople.

The background to this schism was that, although barbarians had for four centuries ruled in Rome, the glamour of her past still gave the city a special authority. This no longer attached to her civil rulers. They were seen by the kings and princes of Europe as men whose ancestors, like their own, had taken power by force of arms and not by legal devolution. It was not they who were the heirs of the mighty Romans of the past. The true heir was the Bishop of Rome, who had assumed the title that emperors had borne—*Pontifex Maximus* or high priest. It was from his person that authority was now seen to flow, and it was his triple crown that radiated the power which once had sparkled from the imperial diadem. Monarchs in the new kingdoms looked to the Pope for leadership as local governors had once looked to the emperor. They recognised his right to support or to take away their authority, and to speak with a voice sanctified not only by his office but by the five centuries of Rome's imperial history.

But this special position of the Pope of Rome could not logically be recognised either by Constantinople or by the eastern lands it ruled. The emperors in that city knew themselves to be the direct successors of the emperors of Rome, and could not accept that the Bishop of Rome (now no more than the capital of a barbarian kingdom) could be other than subordinate to them. This the popes acknowledged, and for many centuries accepted the emperors in Constantinople as their superiors. Nevertheless, as successors of Peter, bathed in the glory that Constantine on the occasion of his *Adventus* into Rome had bestowed upon their see, the Popes saw themselves first as the spiritual, and increasingly as the political, masters of Western Europe. They could not but resent their nominal subordination to the remote emperors in Constantinople.

The Church in Constantinople, established in a city of Constantine's own foundation, saw itself no less as the true heir of the early church and claimed to be the repository of true and orthodox doctrine.

These tensions had been hidden beneath the formal acceptance by the Pope of the superior authority vested in the emperor at Constantinople. However, when Charlemagne took the title of Emperor in the West, there was now an authority within the Pope's own sphere of influence which he could more acceptably recognise as the chief temporal power. The old allegiance to Constantinople was broken. Pope and emperor, in the persons of Leo III and Charlemagne, resumed their ancient relationship in the West. The two churches, of Rome and Constantinople, now developed independently.

The two camps into which Christianity was now so tragically divided both saw themselves as the legitimate legatees of imperial authority and of the true Christian tradition. Both Churches had taken the Gospel into barbarian lands. Pope Gregory of Rome, for example, had sent St Augustine in 597 to the heathen English kingdoms that had been established in Britain. The Metropolitan of the Orthodox Church in Constantinople sent the news of Christ into the eastern lands. One such missionary, St Cyril, (827-69) later carried the message to the Slavs in the unknown land of Scythia, over which the Eagles had never ruled, and took Christianity (and with it literacy) into the heartlands of Russia. To this day the Russian Cyrillic alphabet is a Greek alphabet, modified by time and distance, and an enduring monument to Cyril, whose name it bears.

Both Churches were fully supported by the civil powers of their respective cities. Inevitably the difference in regard to theological jurisdiction led to a conflict between the governments of the two states.

During the early years of the tenth century, Constantinople enjoyed a period of peace, her Empire almost vanished, and she herself lived a withdrawn life within her walls. The politics of an Empire became the politics of a city and the men who bore the ancient title of Augustus were rulers over narrow dominions. But in 963 Nicephorus became emperor and re-awoke some of the glories of the past. At this time the city successfully withstood an attack by the Russians. Men were heartened by the victory and by this new evidence of their city's ancient invincibility. But after the death of Nicephorus, Constantinople returned to the uneventful life she had before pursued.

During the eleventh century a new enemy was on the march —the Seljuk Turks. Instead of concentrating her forces against this new peril, the city dissipated its military power in almost continual civil wars. Finally, in 1071, the then Augustus, Romanus, was defeated by the Turks and his armies over-whelmed. No means were left to resist the victorious advance of the Turkish enemy. They reached the Hellespont and it seemed that Constantinople was once again to face the hard-ship of a long siege.

But at this time Western Christendom (the Latin Christians) had decided to make united war against the Turks. When the Mohammedans had conquered the Holy Land in the seventh century they had acknowledged that within Jerusalem there were places that were holy to the Christian world. They freely allowed Christians to make pilgrimages there. But matters changed when the Egyptians conquered Syria and ill-treated both the Syrian Christians and the pilgrims from western Europe. However, it was the action of the Seljuk Turks in seizing the Holy Land in 1065 and closing it to all pilgrims that moved the Latin Christians to action. At first, their armies acted with more enthusiasm than wisdom. There was little planning and less success. But, in the very year that Romanus was defeated, a Western army had reached the Eastern Empire, and immediately came to the assistance of their Christian brothers, the differences between the Eastern and Western Churches being forgotten in this time of peril. The Turks were driven back from the Hellespont and Constantinople gained a reprieve.

Two years later, Manuel II, Augustus of Constantinople, begged Pope Gregory VII for further aid. The Pope, finally persuaded by Peter the Hermit who had for long been an advocate of a holy war, summoned a conference at Clermont-Ferrand in 1095. There it was agreed that the kingdoms of the West should furnish an army to win back the city of Jerusalem and the Holy Places for Christendom, making a military con-quest of the land in which the Prince of Peace had been born. From the Western lands ruffians and freebooters, kings, knights and commoners, dedicated men and men who were merely thirsty for adventure or loot, camp-followers and vast numbers of eager women, joined together to march across Europe to attack the Saracens who now held the Holy Places. It was one of the most extraordinary movements in the history of Europe. The banners of the armies were blessed and forgiveness of sins was promised to all those who joined in the campaign. The distinction between men of religion and men of war became blurred. The Cross, emblem of Him who had beatified the peacemakers, was painted on the shields and armour of soldiers from Britain, France, Italy and Austria; and the warlike expeditions were named the Crusades, after the Cross that was their emblem.

The immensity of the undertaking was staggering. The theatre of war lay far away and the long journey there was beset by many perils. Because Byzantium lay at the crossroads of Europe and Asia, and because it was a Christian city, it became the natural staging post for the vast armies journeying from the kingdoms of Europe and converging on the Holy Land. For the first time there was direct contact between the descendants of the barbarian conquerors of Rome in the west and Rome's civilised heirs in Constantinople. Franks and Burgundians, Austrians and Anglo-Saxons, gazed with wonder upon the ancient glories of Constantine's city. Even they, tough fighting men that they were, must have been dazzled by the great churches decorated with glittering mosaics, the marbled glory of statuary, the high domes of the buildings, the libraries and treasures that bedecked the city, and the ancient and seemingly invincible walls surounding it.

The first expedition achieved nothing, and out of all those who had set out from the western kingdoms very few reached Constantinople. Then, in 1096, the kingdoms of the West set out on the first properly organised campaign. Among their leaders were Godfrey of Bouillon, Duke of Lorraine and Robert, Duke of Normandy, son of William the Conqueror. It was agreed that the armies should march in five divisions, each of which would proceed independently to Constantinople. By the summer of 1097 the city was crammed with the crusading troops, who successfully fought their first action at Nicaea, which fell to their attack. After a siege of seven months they took Antioch, putting the obstinate inhabitants to the sword. But during the long siege, the morale of the crusaders fell.

Many died through hunger and disease; others deserted, including Peter the Hermit, whose eloquence and enthusiasm had done so much to further the enterprise. Then the survivors in their turn were besieged in Antioch by a Mohammedan army which, grimly sallying from the city, they routed.

The extent of the crusaders' losses by battle, disease and desertion is shown by the fact that over 500,000 had taken part in the campaign against Nicaea, but only 40,000 marched out of Antioch and managed to reach Jerusalem in the summer of 1099.

Weary but resolute, they drove the Saracens out of the town and set up a Christian Kingdom of Jerusalem with Godfrey of Bouillon as king. His brother became Count of Edessa, while Antioch and the lands around it became another Christian dominion. For the next fifty years these Christian kingdoms flourished and the crusade, at an unbelievable cost of human life, had achieved its end.

But Edessa was conquered by the Saracens, who then assembled a vast host for the destruction of the Christian kingdom of Jerusalem. A second crusade was organised and the Western army, under King Louis VII of France and Conrad III of Germany, marched to the rescue in 1147. Manuel, the Augustus in Constantinople was less sympathetic to the crusading cause than his predecessors had been. The armies of the Cross found little welcome within the City and nothing but disaster beyond its walls. Conrad's German forces were almost totally destroyed in a battle with the Saracens. Those who remained made a brave but unsuccessful attempt to take Damascus. A year after setting out with such brave hopes the defeated and pitiful survivors of the armies returned disconsolately to Europe, carrying back stories of the marvels they had seen in the ancient city by the Hellespont.

Meanwhile the great Mohammedan leader Saladin had marched out of Egypt, broken into Palestine, shattered a Christian army at the ancient town of Tiberias and wrested the city of Jerusalem from its isolated garrison in 1187. Once more the Holy Places had been lost to Christendom and the work of Godfrey of Bouillon was undone.

Roused by this calamity, the princes of Europe organised the Third Crusade. Barbarossa, Emperor of Germany, King Philip of France and King Richard the Lionheart of England, led the flower of their armies eastwards. Barbarossa was drowned during the campaign and it was the French and English leaders, commanding the triple army, who captured the city of Acre after a siege of nearly two years. King Philip of France left the campaign; but Richard of England was able to make a successful treaty with Saladin that won for all pilgrims the right to visit Jerusalem without molestation.

In 1204 a new army, largely French, sailed to Venice on its way to Constantinople and the Holy Land. This was the Fourth Crusade, which was to bring bloody disaster to the city of Constantinople.

Venice was by now a great maritime power whose ships dominated the trade of the eastern Mediterranean. The sea was her element and each year the Doge and his colleagues performed the ceremony of dropping a golden ring into the waters, symbolising the marriage of Venice to the sea. But though she commanded the sea-routes to the east, and although her freighted ships sailed freely to Greece and to all parts of the Levant, she had to recognise the dominant position of the great city on the Hellespont, through which alone trade with Asia could be effectively transacted. It was more to her interest to arrange the destruction of Constantinople (thereby increasing her own mercantile might) than to accomplish the liberation of the far-off Holy Places of Jerusalem, which played no part in her commercial affairs.

She was too small a power to wage a campaign against her rival. But if she could divert the army of the Fourth Crusade to attack Constantinople, her aim would be achieved by the swords of others. The task was not difficult. The Crusaders as always had set out as much for adventure as for religion, and looked forward to booty nearly as fervently as they looked for the success of their mission. Some had seen and all had heard of the wealth of Constantinople. The possibility of enriching themselves with booty made them an easy prey to the persuasions of Venice.

The Doge of Venice, Enrice Dandolo, a blind old man whose political skill was undiminished by age, negotiated skilfully with the French army. They needed ships from the Venetians to make their journey to the Holy Land and the Doge made them an attractive offer of help. Venice would provide all the ships and provisions necessary for their armies, together with transports for the horses. She would also furnish a squadron of fifty fighting ships. In return the crusaders were to pay a substantial sum of money before sailing and were to divide with Venice any booty or conquests that they made. Having thus obtained the gratitude of the French, the Venetians now sought a pretext to attack their rival.

Constantinople was suffering one of those struggles for power that had become so tragically familiar. Isaac II, brother of the emperor Alexius, had declared himself Augustus. Alexius left the city as a fugitive and escaped to Macedonia. There his brother Isaac caused him to be blinded and kept him as a prisoner. Alexius's son, also called Alexius, was twelve years old at the time and escaped into Italy. There he learned of the assembling of the French crusaders, whom he and his advisers saw as a likely instrument for the destruction of his uncle, Isaac, and for his own appointment as Augustus.

The Doge of Venice grasped the opportunity offered by the young imperial exile and espoused his cause. It was thus as the liberators of Constantinople from the tyranny of Isaac Augustus and as rescuers of a wronged prince that the Venetian fleet sailed in 1204 in a mighty armada of nearly 500 ships.

Voyaging across the Adriatic, the knights and men-at-arms eagerly awaited the onset of battle. Although their avowed purpose had been the defeat of the unbelievers in the Holy Land, their swords and spears were now directed against their fellow Christians in Constantinople. The blind Doge of Venice, clad in full armour, stood at the prow of his ship as the fleet moved in to the shore. Constantinople mustered no fleet to fight them at sea and made but poor resistance on land. The city's best defence was offered not by the citizens of her Empire but by the mercenary guards, Englishmen and Danes, who had enlisted in the Emperor's army. But neither their constancy nor their

terrible battleaxes were enough to defend the city, which fell
to the combined French and Venetian armies in 1204.

Constantinople had suffered defeat before, but no army had
treated this Christian city as savagely as did the Christian army
of the west. It endured not only the humiliation of defeat but
great slaughter and merciless pillage. The citizens suffered more
from the swords and spears of their fellow Christians than ever
they had from the scimitars of the Turks or Saracens. Constantinople now had to suffer the same horrors Rome had known
some 400 years earlier. Men were butchered and, despite orders
to spare nuns, married women and virgins, women were raped.
The churches were ransacked, their treasures looted; the
ancient and learned libraries were pillaged; the palaces sacked.
Yet out of this tragedy, and out of the irony of the slaughter of
Christian by Christian, something of the spirit of ancient Rome
was revived and what Alaric had destroyed was, by this new
destruction, in part rebuilt. The rich loot of Constantinople was
carried by the knights and men-at-arms first into Italy and
thence into all the nations of Europe. The gardens of princes
and nobles were embellished with classical statues. The libraries
of the aristocracy acquired precious manuscripts containing the
forgotten learning of the ancient world.

The intellectual horizons of Europe began to be enlarged.
As so often happens in human affairs, conflict between two
societies leads to closer (though hostile) contact. When the
West and Constantinople had been content to go their separate
ways, the links between them had grown attenuated and the
two cultures increasingly divergent.

In western Europe the memory of Rome was vanishing.
True, Charlemagne had conjured up its ghost. But the nations
of the West had inherited far more from their barbarian fore-
bears than from their scarce-remembered imperial predecessors.
Government was by warlike kings, not by consul or consistory.
A barbarian (or gothic) civilisation flourished, with the battlefield almost the only place where esteem might be won and
the Church the only patron of the arts. The tranquil and
idealised realism of classical sculpture had yielded place to the
grotesque, or to the vigorous but sterner sculpture of the

North, where the carved wooden crucifixes depicted the human sufferings of Christ rather than His divine attributes.

Now that war had brought the vigorous new culture into direct conflict with the isolated heirs of the ancient world, men's minds in the West began to develop a new interest and a curiosity about the past. The storming of Constantinople was not enough to bring this to final fruition. But it was a significant beginning. Dante was born a mere fifty years later and could take Augustus's poet Virgil as his master. Petrarch translated the works of Homer from Greek into Latin. The world of the Caesars was re-awakening. From Florence, Giacomo da Scaparia visited Constantinople to study Greek. A department of Greek studies was formed in the University of Florence and thereafter the Gothic cultures of Europe began rapidly to change.

Forgotten books were once again remembered. Out of the darkness of the past, Christian Europe had been content to receive only two books as important—the Bible and the writings of Aristotle. These two works were the source of all knowledge; but they also represented the frontier set for curiosity, beyond which it was improper for the human mind to range. The forgotten poets of Rome, with their mixture of ribaldry and wisdom, of eroticism and urbanity, were once more read. Juvenal and Horace, Lucretius with his deep curiosity about the structure of the universe, Ovid with his springtime voice and his landscape embroidered with bright blossom and winding rivers, Virgil who had celebrated the greatness of Rome's beginnings—all these slowly came back into the knowledge of Europe, whose peoples had before lost sight of this part of their heritage.

But for Constantinople, the break with the past created by Alaric and his soldiers during those six summer days of 410 might have been total. No other memorial would have been left in Europe of Rome's greatness other than the ruined buildings scattered across the continent, and the broken roads, long fallen into disrepair, along which trade travelled and armies marched. But now there came about a rebirth of learning, a renaissance of interest in the elegant arts of Greece and the civilising practicality of Rome. Michelangelo, Francis Bacon, Shakespeare and the other figures of the Renaissance could not have worked but for the accident of history that led Constantine to build a new Rome in the safety of Asia Minor. There, far from the western and northern barbarians who destroyed the Empire and who brought their alien and lower standards to the lands where Rome had ruled, Constantinople held safe the treasures of the ancient world.

She herself was not immortal. She finally fell (her last Augustus, Constantine XI, dying with her) to the Mohammedans in 1453. But she had been true to her trust for 1,000 years, trustee of the old world. The overthrow of Constantinople gave the final stimulus to the Renaissance. Fleeing from the Mohammedan conquerors, scholars and learned men came to Western Europe, bringing with them the manuscripts and knowledge of the ancient world. Once more Roman plays were read, and once more columns and colonnades were used in the building of a new and more urbane Europe. More and more the dialectic of Greek writers like Plato, the careful sense of history of men like Herodotus, and the scientific approach to the external world of Lucretius, and of his predecessors the Ionian philosophers, began to be revealed and understood. A new hunger for knowledge, a new thirst for beauty and a new passion of curiosity, came into men's minds. These emotions were not new but were a re-awakening of the forgotten motives that had taken the armies of Rome to the limits of Europe and had built a unified and enduring empire. So the boast of the Romans, that theirs was an Eternal City, proved in the end to be true, despite Rome's fall.

To recognise Rome as one of the most important sources of western civilisation is to realise the greatness of the men at whose lives we have glanced. Julius Caesar, for all his ruthlessness and brutality, laid the foundations of permanence upon which others could build. Augustus, with his political subtlety and caution, developed the concept of a responsible ruler to whom men might look for stability and justice. The modesty and austerity of his life, which left its mark in the traditions of Rome, defended Europe by making the over-

N

weening tyranny of monarchs unacceptable. The development of a civil service under Claudius and others, the common sense of Vespasian, the fine virtues of Trajan, Hadrian, Antoninus Pius and Marcus Aurelius, gave shining examples to subsequent rulers of the new kingdoms. These proved more enduring than the aberrations of Caligula or the excesses of Elagabalus.

The soldier emperors of the fourth century, Alexander Severus, Diocletian, Maximianus and Constantius Chlorus, imposed upon Europe the tradition that all rulers were military men, and that the sword is as much a mark of the monarch as is the sceptre. Kings, even those few who are left, are still identified with the military power, and military or naval dress is still the mark of princes. This is a heritage that has proved less profitable than Rome's other legacies.

But in the end it was not Rome's soldiers who secured the survival of her culture. In their day they were invincible, but when night came they proved mortal and perished. It was the patient work of the Caesars, each for good or for evil contributing something of his own personality to the total conception of the Empire, which gave it solidity and endurance. Julius Caesar had demonstrated the unity of Europe and Claudius the wisdom of establishing a system of ministers to advise and work for the occupant of the throne. The Antonines showed that virtue could be the companion of authority.

The ruffianly Carausius gave the island of Britain its first taste of independence as a nation state. The soldier emperors of Illyria had shown what resolution could achieve in preserving the ancient orders. Postumus had proved that the Atlantic provinces possessed an inherent unity. But most of all, it was the sound wisdom of Diocletian, who saw clearly the logical division between East and West, and the providence of Constantine, who stored in a second and safer capital both the physical treasures and the treasures of the mind, which ensured the survival of Rome's influence, together with the beauty, elegance and logic of Greece, which Rome had so admired and defended.

SOURCE
MATERIAL

For Julius Caesar's campaigns in Gaul and Britain, and for his
wars against Pompey, we have his own first-hand accounts
in his two books *De Bello Gallico* and *De Bello Civile*. Both
of these are available in the Penguin Classics, translated by
Jane F. Mitchell, with most informative introductions and
notes. Plutarch, who was born about AD 40, wrote the *Lives*
of forty-six eminent Greeks and Romans. His accounts of
Julius Caesar, Mark Antony and others contain much useful
material.

Gaius Suetonius Tranquillus (born about AD 70) wrote the
lives of Julius Caesar and of his eleven successors. I have made
extensive use of this material for all the Caesars from Julius
to Domitian. Suetonius, an ardent republican, wrote with a
political purpose in mind, namely to show the vice and corruption that inevitably attend upon absolute power placed
in the hands of individuals. His book must therefore be read
with caution. His work, in Robert Graves' lively translation,
is also available in the Penguin Classics.

The same period is covered by that great historian Cornelius
Tacitus (c AD 55-120). His *Agricola* (the life of his famous
father-in-law) contains precious information about the conquest of Britain. His *Annales* and *Historiae*, both alas incom-
plete, furnish excellent material from the death of Augustus

to the death of Nero and for the Caesars from Galba to Domitian.

Accounts of all the Caesars from Hadrian down to Numerian are to be found in the *Historia Augusta*, a work compiled by six authors writing towards the end of the third century and the beginning of the fourth. These authors, Aelius Spartianus, Julius Capitolinus, Vulcacius Gallicanus, Aelius Lampridius, Trebellius Pollio and Flavius Vopiscus, embellished their work with a considerable amount of fiction and legend. The text is available in the Loeb Classical Library, with a translation by David Magie. Doctor Magie's annotations lead one carefully through the thickets of legend and give illuminating cross-references to the works of other authors, to inscriptions and to coins.

The Greek historian Cassius Dio was born in the eastern Empire c 155. His *History of Rome* covers the period from the legendary days of Aeneas to 229. It is excellent material, but the greater part of the text has unfortunately been lost.

Eusebius wrote a life of Constantine (*De Vita Constantini*), which provides invaluable information, as do the writings of Lactantius (*De Mortibus Persecutorum*).

The Greek writer Herodian (who flourished c 250) wrote a history of the Empire from the times of Marcus Aurelius down to the period of the Gordians. His works are available in the Loeb Classical Library, edited and translated by C. R. Whittaker.

Also in the Loeb Classical Library, translated by John C. Rolfe, are the works of Ammianus Marcellinus, who was born c 330 in Antioch, and who wrote a history of the descendants and successors of Constantine down to Valens.

I have made abundant use of the information provided by the Roman coinage, partly from the coins in my own collection (the bulk of which was unfortunately stolen some years ago), and partly from *Roman Coins and Their Values* by David R. Sear, published by B. A. Seaby Ltd. This contains an extremely full list of the inscriptions on the imperial coinage and many illustrations, some of which are reproduced in this book with the kind permission of David Sear.

I have also made use of the summary history of the Caesars written by Sextus Aurelius Victor (*De Vita et Moribus Imperatorum*), which covers all the Caesars from Augustus to Theodosius. Also, I have used *Romanae Historiae Compendium* (from Gordian to Justinian and his successors) written by Pomponius Laetus.

Of later writers, Egnazio wrote a useful short account of all the Caesars from Julius Caesar down to the Byzantine Emperors.

Edward Gibbons' *The Decline and Fall of the Roman Empire* is an invaluable secondary source. Professor A. H. M. Jones's *The Later Roman Empire* is an indispensable guide to the period from 284. His very full notes contain abundant texts from important source material.

Also, I have used *Constantine* by Ramsay Macmullen (Weidenfeld & Nicolson, 1969) and *Julius Caesar* by Alfred Duggan (Faber & Faber, 1955). Both give excellent accounts of their subjects.

The coin portraits in this book are reproduced from *Roman Coins and Their Values* by David R. Sear (published by B. A. Seaby Ltd), with the author's kind permission.

Page	Left	Right
13	Julius Caesar	Augustus
44	Tiberius	Nero
76	Trajan	Hadrian
106	Maximinus	Philip
139	Diocletian	Constantine the Great

INDEX

NEW ROCHELLE PUBLIC LIBRARY

3 1019 15147124 3

9/23/92 last page ripped out